M.S.

My Story

Where it all began

Foreword

It is with great honor and admiration that I introduce Nicole Tracey and her incredible work on mindset and lifestyle for those living with Multiple Sclerosis (MS). As a passionate advocate and a valued member of our Facebook group dedicated to MS and fitness, Nicole has consistently inspired us with her tenacity and positive outlook on life.

With over 45 years of experience in the fitness industry, and as a proud inductee of the National Fitness Hall of Fame, I understand firsthand the vital role that mindset plays in achieving our health and wellness goals. After my own diagnosis of MS in 2006, more than 18 years ago, I have witnessed the profound impact that a positive approach can have on navigating this journey.

In her book, Nicole dives deep into the experience of living with MS, sharing her personal insights and practical strategies that empower individuals to take control of their health and mindset. She masterfully combines her expertise as a blogger for our MS Fitness Challenge charity with her own life lessons, creating a roadmap for resilience and hope.

Nicole's dedication transcends mere advocacy; she embodies the spirit of community and support that we often seek when faced with the challenges of MS. Her writing is not just informative; it resonates with authenticity and heart, making it accessible to anyone navigating their own path with this condition.

Whether you are newly diagnosed, a long-time warrior, or a caregiver, Nicole's words will guide you toward a more fulfilling lifestyle-one rooted in strength, self-compassion, and a positive mindset. This book is not just about managing a diagnosis; it's about thriving despite it.

Join me in celebrating Nicole's efforts to bring light and encouragement to those affected by MS. I encourage you to embrace the wisdom within these pages and take the steps toward a lifestyle that honors your journey.

In Health,

David Lyons, MS Advocate

Founder www.MSFitnessChallenge.org

Creator of OptimalBody Fitness www.obpfitness.com

(David Lyons, receiving the Health Advocate Lifetime Acheivement Award from Arnold Schwarzennegger in 2015)

This book is dedicated to my Mom, who taught me that you can lose yourself in a story, if it's the right one.

Acknowledgments

I have a few people that I need to acknowledge. I hope you will indulge me.....these people are very special to me. The first three are my sons from oldest to youngest. They are what drives me forward every day.

To Carson - For always believing in me, and shouldering the burden of worry so well

To Nolan - Who has always been my shoulder to cry on, and my "go-to" guy. I could always count on you.

To Emerson - For always helping without complaint, for putting a hand on my shoulder when I needed one, and for being my source of calm when I've had enough.

To my sister: Always....... just a phone call away.

To my husband -Who started me on the path to looking towards natural solutions and who has always been my one true love.

To Mama P - for always being my ear

David and Kendra Lyons - For dedicating your life to helping people see that their body can shine if given the right tools

My love to all

Dearest reader: I hope you find this book to be an uplifting, quick read that makes you realize that you can want for a better life in spite of that scary diagnosis, and that it is possible to get there just by giving the body what it needs. It is possible to change your outcome.

This book is not intended to diagnose or to act as a prescription to treat a condition, it is simply my story, and how my life has transpired thus far.

I wrote this book when my life was still impacted by MS. Be forewarned that there may be a few swear words peppering my story......but they're just words, so I hope it doesn't offend anyone too much, and you can enjoy the content as it is.

With positivity and gratitude, it is possible to push through the adversity and strife in your life.

You're about to read my Superhero story.

Nicole Tracey

Contents Page

11. My Story
49. Mind over Matter
58. Nick's Journal Notes
90. My Daily Template
95. Self-care and Self-talk
107. Munchie Go-to's
111. Give Thanks
118. Continuing the Journey
137. Food For Thought-Are you going to eat that?
146. Naughty and Nice Recipes

Started book Oct. 4th, 2022

Where do I start?

   Well....I guess I'll take you back to the year 2013.

It began with my vision.

I knew deep down that what I was experiencing was something serious because it came on so suddenly.

It's hard to describe, but I'll try.

Snowballs of light blocked my ability to read numbers or text clearly. There was a strange shimmery glow around objects. This became really concerning to me because I'd always heard that if your vision suddenly changes.....it's bad. It affected my everyday. I even had trouble reading stoplights. The red and yellow lights that dictate our driving were almost invisible to me. I almost had to look peripherally to know what colour the light was, because when I looked at it straight on....it was like they were indistinguishable. I couldn't see the light until I was almost right on top of it. Funny....the green were usually ok.

That was scary as hell.

Also, have you ever had your foot fall asleep? ....You know, when your foot falls asleep but if you walk around on it a bit and get the blood flowing, it goes away. This wasn't like that. It was constant. It was happening all down the right side of my body. That's not normal. This was very troubling to me, as it not only inhibited my sleep, it scared the shit out of me. It was another big symptom that further highlighted that something major was going on with me.

These health issues were affecting my work. Numbers became more difficult to decipher. I had a hard time distinguishing between certain numbers like 3, 5, and 8. This was alarming to me as I was Customer Service at a large manufacturing company, and if I couldn't see or read the orders the customers wanted, it was some serious shit.

What could be happening to me?

I was so afraid. Was it cancer? A tumor pressing on some deep optic nerve behind my eyes?

I remember all the specialists' appointments I had in rapid succession-optometrists, ophthalmologists, and neurologists.....oh my!

When the symptoms affect your vision, life gets real right quick.

It wasn't a muscle cramp that I could power through, it was my vision! We need sight for everything we do. It was a scary time for me and my family.

2013 is the year my life was altered by the diagnosis of Multiple Sclerosis (MS)

~

I had three small children. They didn't know what MS was, or how it was going to affect their little lives.

I didn't even know how it was going to impact my own life. Would I be in a wheelchair? Would I die young? Would I get to see my boys grow up?

I was a factory worker; I had zero savings in the bank to deal with any sort of time away from work if my health decided to take a turn. This weighed heavily on my mind. I was already living paycheck to paycheck, struggling to pay the bills, get groceries and keep my family of five fed, let alone worry about what this disease might do to my health.

Up until this point in my life, I had not made any connection or put any thought into how trauma, stress, what we eat, how much water we drink, the happiness that surrounds us, or the lack of any of the above may have played a part in why I may have developed multiple sclerosis.

Trauma and stress...check.

I grew up in a stress-filled home, with loving but alcoholic parents; not enough money, and all the baggage that comes with that.

It was the 70's, and in my family at least, children should be heard but not seen. As long as my parents heard us playing somewhere in the neighbourhood they didn't worry. Our days started after school on the weekdays and the moment we arose on the weekends, and as long as we were in when the streetlights came on, all was well.

I recall many a night falling asleep to the sound of my mother's raucous, jovial voice coming up through the heating vent, because my parents were entertaining company. We lived in an old house, the type where you could hear everything through the heating vents......oh yeah, remind me to tell you a spooky story involving my sister and said heating vents when I'm done with my little introduction here!

Many a night, I would grab my parents an extra beer, just so we could stay at my cousin's house a little longer.....but I also remember worrying a lot as a child. That takes a toll on your health, I would imagine. Worrying over whether or not your Father or Mother just got another drink at the family wedding you're attending, and that they still have to drive home... *because you can tell just enough as a little kid to know they shouldn't.* Or worry that your parents will die young because they smoke and drink to excess, and then who knows what would happen to you because you're just a little kid.

As a kid, I never questioned my parents love.

We were taught morals, integrity, and right from wrong. They did the best for us they knew how.

Okay ...I didn't forget about that spooky story!

I was about six or seven years old, and my sister and I used to share a room. It was a fairly large room with a chunky, brown 70's style bunkbed, a worn grey carpet with faded red lillies, and a large plywood desk that ran the length of the room. I remember loving that desk because my Father built it for us, although it was made with that picky plywood, probably because it was cheaper for him to make. It sometimes gave me slivers because he didn't have time to smooth it out, it was probably all he could do to put it up for us. He worked really, really long hours at an industrial equipment supplier. I vividly remember sitting at our beautiful, picky desk with a tape recorder and trying to learn the words to Dolly Parton and John Mellencamp songs with my sister.

I can only imagine what we put my mother through, with two young girls in the same space. Especially since I used to crawl down to my sister's bed almost every night because I was afraid to sleep in the top bunk by myself. (which in retrospect, was probably not the smartest place for me to begin with, as I was prone to seizures.)

My sister Tricia and I are two years apart. I feel like my Mom had finally had enough...she decided to separate us. She moved my sister to the basement. Do you remember me mentioning how old the house was? This is where it gets good. I honestly can't remember if it was at my sister's request, or if my Mom just separated us because she couldn't take it anymore.

It didn't help that I used to pee the bed almost every night. Well, more like, I used to pee in my sister's bed since I used to crawl down there every night. I recall having a recurring dream around this young age where I would go down the hall to the bathroom to relieve the urge, and when I got to the toilet, I would literally touch the toilet in my dream, and say "Yup, this is real...I can feel the toilet" and then I would turn around, sit on it, start to urinate - and that is when I would be awakened by the warm sensation on my thigh. This could have been a catalyst for the big move too, now that I think about it.

Maybe my sister didn't want to get peed on anymore.

We changed a lot of sheets. I also remember staying up well past my bedtime many nights, giggling and laughing with my sister, when we should have been fast asleep.

O.k, shut up Nick, and tell the story......

Tricia's basement room reminded me of where Nosferatu might have kept his casket. There was absolutely **no** warmth in our basement. A cement, spiral staircase led to a large open tomb...err, I mean room with a low ceiling. Cold, grey cinderblock walls greeted us everywhere we looked. Not a strip of fabric anywhere. My sister's room was in a far corner on the right hand side of our old dingy basement. It was not an ideal room for a little girl.

I was lost without Tricia.

I was so scared being by myself. As my mom put me to bed that first night, I couldn't believe I was in my big bedroom all alone. I didn't know what to do without my sister. After my mom went back downstairs, **I had an idea**....I crawled over to the heating grate whispering into it so my mother wouldn't hear me.

.""Triii-sshaa........Triiissshaa......"Triiiissshaa........"

Down in the basement, all my sister could hear was this ghostly voice saying her name over and over in the dark... having no idea it was her petrified sister three flights up.

Needless to say we were not separated for long.

Fast forward to my early adulthood, and I'll be the first to admit that the choices I made during that time were definitely questionable. As a teenager and into my early adulthood, I punished my body with alcohol, fast food, cigarettes, and lack of sleep.

~

One night while doing just that at my friends house, she decided she wanted to set me up with *her* friend. He was a country boy, and I was a city gal, but we hit it off. We started dating.

He didn't have a car, so he would hitchhike whenever we wanted to meet up. I remember meeting at McDonald's all the time. It's funny, even though he hitchhiked all the way from the county (about half hour away), he would give me a time to meet at McDonalds, and he was usually pretty accurate even though he had to bum a ride. He always got picked up pretty quick...... so I never usually had to wait long.

After a while of dating, and hitch-hiking to see each other, he finally bought a truck, and we were able to get together more regularly. No more clandestine meet-ups at McDee's!

We were together for six years, and did some pretty exciting things together. We took a scuba diving course, and drove all the way to Ohio to get certified. He was better at it than me.....I always had a hard time clearing my ears. We went on a scuba/camping trip to Tobermory, Ontario and we dove on some shipwrecks....that was cool.

In my early twenties, I had an opportunity to buy my first house. That'll grow you up quick...having a mortgage.

I purchased my house on my own.

A little source of pride as I was only 23. Working swing shift at the factory wasn't great pay, but it was steady. This allowed me to go to the bank and show that I had the means to pay a small mortgage. It also helped that I bought my first house from my sister. It was very cheap and I couldn't pass it up.

Now, I had been with my boyfriend for about five years at this time......but with my newfound responsibility as a homeowner, we slowly started to drift apart, because I think it made me grow up a bit faster. I remember the years previous and I would see some of our mutual friends get engaged and always wondered when and if he would propose to me.

He chose Christmas 1997.

I'm sure proposing is a little stressful for a man. People always want to hear the story of the proposal, so it has to be good. He even did the chivalrous thing and asked my Father if he could have his daughter's hand in marriage.

It was our first Christmas in my new house, and we had opened all of our Christmas gifts. That's when he told me that he thought there was a still a gift under there....a small box. It was hidden behind the post of the tree.

I was with my boyfriend for a long time, and always thought I wanted him to propose...until I saw that little wrapped box. Then, my first thought was.....

"Well, this is it? Do I really want to marry this guy?"

Falling back on the familiar, I said yes.

Around the same time, I met Jason. We both worked in the same manufacturing facility, and we grew close...rather quickly.

He was unlike anyone I had ever known-smart, good-looking, and funny as hell. Humour and intelligence are so attractive to me.

Even though I was engaged to my fiance, Jason's and my friendship blossomed. We were good friends first; a relationship that grew because we worked three feet from each other-all day long. Our co-workers used to think that I was cheating on my fiance with Jason since we got along exceptionally well. We worked so close together, it was almost inevitable that we would become more than friends. We talked about our hopes and dreams, movies, and miscellaneous.... mundane stuff that I had been starved for because I wasn't getting that in my current relationship. My fiancé's idea of talking was asking for the TV remote.

I remember going out for lunch with my sister, and I confided in her that I thought I was falling for Jason......the more I worked with him, the more I began to question my current relationship. I was just way more compatible with Jason. I started to enjoy going into work because I got to work three feet from this intelligent, good-looking man, who loved to play word games with me. That made the workday go by so quickly. Really, you had to do something to keep yourself mentally stimulated as you performed the same motion over and over for eight hours. It was factory work; it was not that exciting.....but *Jason* made going into work exciting! But back to my previous relationship. I broke off my engagement in June, after watching an episode of Oprah and the funny thing was I didn't normally watch Oprah. But when I heard her description of the episode, I couldn't keep scrolling anymore. She had me hooked and I had to see what it was about.

If I remember correctly, it was about big life altering decisions, like making sure you are with the right person. I recall one of her guests had called off her wedding years before. It turned out that it was the right decision for her.

It just hit me the right way, talking about happiness and if you were sure you were with the person you were meant to be with. And it is true what they say, every break up begins with the phrase... "We need to talk." (That's exactly what I said to my fiance the night I broke up with him.)

That episode of Oprah made me think of the what if's.

I recollect, the night after watching that Oprah episode, driving to my parents' house and telling my mom that I was in love with another man, and that I didn't want to get married.

We had just picked out my wedding dress a few months before. The hall was booked, a date picked, and invitations sent. My mother was supportive of my feelings and asked a lot of questions about this new man in my life. I think she could tell I was serious, and I feel like a part of her didn't want me to go through with the marriage if I was already questioning it. I remember my Dad, on the other hand, being really upset with me, because I had been with my current fiancé for six years. He might have thought his youngest daughter was being a floozy, or acting in a rash way just because I met a new exciting man.

In truth, I had envisioned a life with my current fiance and I had to ask myself, "Will you be happy in 25 years?"

I knew instinctively that the answer was no.

So, I broke it off.

That was hard. One of the hardest decisions I ever had to make. I wasn't discarding our past six years callously. I just didn't want to wake up one day regretting the last quarter century of my life because I married someone I was no longer compatible with.

I wanted more, and I knew he could never give me that. I think my priorities had changed since purchasing a house. I was now a home owner, I had responsibilities, bills......grass to cut! I gave his ring back and he moved out.

It didn't take long for me to grow close with Jason.

I remember mine and Jason's first date vividly, and me running around my tiny war-time home getting ready. I was super excited that our relationship had taken that romantic turn, and he was coming to my house to pick me up...because we had a date. A date!!! Oh my God!

Butterflies filled my stomach just thinking about it. I hadn't been on a date in over six years, so it was new and exciting......a date with a new man, someone who was also a wonderful friend. I had never experienced that before. All of my previous boyfriends were set-up as blind dates by friends. This was new and fun and exciting!

Not only was Jason funny, he was so smart. We used to read Trivial Pursuit cards at work. He floored me with his intelligence and knowledge of things.

We worked together at this big machine that cut four lengths of webbing at a time for seatbelts. I would pull them off the webcutter, hold them, and then wait for four more pieces to come down the trough and when I had eight, I would roll them, and put them in a box. (while I was rolling my eight, Jason would grab the next four pieces.....he would pull it off the webcutter, hold them and wait for four more, and then roll them and put them in the box. The machine went pretty quick though.....there was not many seconds in between cuts, so you had to roll fast. We'd take turns doing that over and over for a full 8-hour workday. One day Jason and I were standing there working, and he was more quiet than usual.

In factory work, if the person you're working with doesn't talk, it can get boring really quick. I kept pestering him to tell me what was wrong....when finally he spilled it.

What he said gives me chills to this day.

He told me he couldn't stop thinking about me. He told me that I was the first thing he thought of the moment he woke up, and the last thing he thought about before going to bed.

Whoa....that did it.

Jason and I quickly went from friends, to more than friends. After a respectable six months, he moved in with me, and because of our minimal responsibility and our desire to spend time together, we ate out.... A LOT. We ate out almost every week. We discovered this fancy restaurant downtown, and became frequent customers. It was a place that used a lot of cream and butter. My diet was unhealthy to say the least, and I quickly gained weight and ballooned to 200lbs.

Working midnights, it's easier for sleep to become optional. Midnight shifts are terrible for that; humans are a diurnal creature - meaning of, or during the day. Fast food became my meal of choice. It gets addictive after a while......the Golden Arches are a quarter of a billion dollar company for a reason! That's another poor decision stemming from lack of sleep......I didn't want to cook. It became another chore. Combine my incredibly inadequate diet with my nicotine habit and I was on the fast track to major health issues. Aaah...the bliss of youth. Pepsi became my go-to drink. This went on for about four solid years.

When we're young, we feel like we're invincible. Truth was, I was damaging my body, and laying the groundwork for disease to take hold due to my many years of yoyo dieting and fast food binges.

Jason was dealing with his own major health issue at this time.

He was experiencing horrible headaches that would literally wake him up at night. From what I've learned......headaches should *never* wake you from sleep. His mom being an emergency room nurse, convinced him to go to the ER on a night she was working. He did, thankfully.

Soon after triaging him and after a CAT scan to see what was causing his headaches, it was determined that Jason would not be going home that night. On his scan.....Jason had two large aneurysms and what looked like a network of spaghetti in his brain.

The medical term for what he had was an AVM (Arteriovenous Malformation) Wow.

I recall going home, calling my mom, sobbing and asking her if she was contagious. Seriously. {She had had aneurysms a couple of years before, and had them successfully removed.} I can't win the lottery, but both my mother and my boyfriend needing invasive brain surgery......well, it was almost too much for me to comprehend.

What are the fucking odds?!

Jason was facing the terrifying thought of someone cutting a hole in his skull with a saw, the real possibility that he was about to unravel the mysteries of death, and the sudden knowledge that this may be the end of us.....so he decided he wanted to propose.

Unbeknownst to me, he had his mother pick up a ring while he was in the hospital. (Ironically, we had browsed rings a few weeks before, so he knew what I liked.) Late January was the date for Jason's surgery.......SPOILER ALERT!!.....Thanks to an incredible team of surgeons, he made it through the surgery with flying colours, and over the next several weeks continued to heal in hospital.

In February, he was released and came home to fully recover. I was still working at this point (......someone had to pay the bills right?)

Jason was home recovering, so he had the opportunity to covertly plan his proposal. He just had brain surgery three weeks before, so he wasn't doing his own shopping. Enlisting the help of his mom once again.....he went at it.

 It was Valentine's Day.

When I got home, he pulled me in, sat me down, and handed me a series of clues written on red paper hearts.

Our little card table was set in the middle of our big old entryway. We didn't have a lot of money, so we didn't have the proper furniture to fill the space. We lived in a house built in the 1920's, and it had a rather large entryway with an oak staircase and hardwood floors. Our little card table was set up for dinner. Table cloth, candles, wine, chicken piccata....(I was not a PBV then...plant based vegan)

I then had to search all over the house. Each clue netted me my favourites.....rum butter lifesavers......Rain-Blo Jumbo gum......salt water taffy......(wonder why my dentist loved me), but when I got to the final clue he took the red paper heart from my hand and replaced it with his own. He got down on bended knee and asked me to be his wife.

I was going to be a Mrs.....Holy Shit.

We were engaged for two years prior to getting married. Every bride wants to be beautiful for her big day, so of course I wanted to lose weight for our upcoming wedding. I did it by taking a medicine prescribed by my doctor that limited the amount of fat you could have in a given day....the only downfall....if you ate too much fat ....you shit yourself.

That particular side effect was enough to keep me on track.

We had our wedding, and went off on our honeymoon. Jamaica. You live what you know..... I had been there on vacation with my globe-trotting, travel agent sister. I would choose Ireland now; it's more to my tastes but when you're young, you stick with the familiar. I gained 8lbs in the two weeks we were enjoying our newfound nuptials. I'm sure it had nothing to do with all of that delicious Jamaican Coco bread or the lavish food layouts at mealtime.

After our honeymoon, we immediately went to work trying to get pregnant. It didn't take long.... three months after our wedding, I was with child. We would have made the baby boomers proud!

I used my early pregnancy as an excuse to eat anything I fancied, partially because I was a new mother and partially because the moment I found out, I quit smoking. So because of that, I was rapidly putting the weight back on! I think I may have had undiagnosed preeclampsia with my firstborn. I was retaining so much water during that pregnancy,. I would take off my shoes after an 8-hour shift, and my ankles were three times their normal size. I remember, in my last trimester, craving some watermelon, so I indulged at my leisure. It's just watermelon....what's the harm right?! It's a fruit for God Sakes!!!

That week at my obstetrician's appointment I had gained 8 lbs!! In a week! I recall the nurse doing a double take at the scale and checking my weight a couple of times. I can imagine what ran through her head. That's impressive to gain that much weight in that short of a period of time. (Google Credit: Sumo wrestlers usually only aspire to gain 1-2lbs a week. 8lbs is legendary levels!) Poe would have been proud. Sorry, had to throw in a little Kung-Fu Panda reference...it's one of my faves!

At my highest weight during my first pregnancy, I was 279 lbs! My husband enjoys watching football, and I knew the starting weight of, say, a linebacker had to be in line with my current weight..... so I asked him how much a full grown man in that position typically weighs and it was only then that

I found out that I was HEAVIER than a linebacker on a football team!

I can also recall, at my first baby shower, wearing a dress that was one of the largest pieces of material I'd ever seen! Dark blue with little white flowers. The designers of this particular pattern probably thought the abundance of flowers would distract the eye from the fact that I was *oh so* large and in charge.

Ugh. It didn't work. I looked like I was wearing a circus tent.

Anyway, I gave birth to my first son who was a whopping 10lb 11oz! (Yay, I really only weighed 268 lbs!) I then proceeded to lose 44 lbs of water weight over the next couple of <u>days</u>.....I didn't know the body could drain that fast!

But, I held on to most of my pregnancy weight like it was an old friend and got pregnant with my second child. We wanted our kids to be close......like two years apart. We pictured them being closer as brothers if they were closer in age. So..... along comes baby #2.

Due to the increased activity of chasing after a little one and caring for a newborn, I was able to shed some, but not all of the baby weight I had gained for my second. I retain the memory of standing at my counter doing dishes one day after I gave birth, and I had this odd tingle that ran from the base of my neck to the small of my back. I learned later that was one of my body's subtle warning signs that disease had been born. I just didn't know it yet.

I wish my Mom was alive when I was diagnosed. She would have comforted me in a way only a Mother could...but I'll take you back a little bit...

In 2005, my Mother had been dealing with her own battle with lung cancer. I researched all kinds of different ways to treat it, trying to get her home care, and just attempting to get her to take some action towards the monster she was dealing with. Little did I know that the doctors had given her six short months to live, so all of my efforts were in vain. She had already made up her mind she was going to die. There was no fight left in her......She died February 24th, 2006.

My Mom had a hard life. Very fucking hard. And her reward? Lung cancer. She only had 61 years on this earth. So young......too young. I wish she could have lived long enough to come visit me in Prince Edward Island, a calm, pretty island I call home now. She would have loved it.....and she would also have loved that I was not tied to an interest rate anymore. My parents always struggled because money was tight....so I know she would be so happy.

My Mother was an intelligent, creative, caring person. She taught me a love of books. She wanted to be a teacher, as she loved children. She would have made an incredible teacher. I have a distant memory of being in a classroom with her when she was substitute teaching. She must have not been able to find a babysitter for me that particular day, and this was well before you needed to spend thirty thousand dollars on education to be a teacher. She gave up her dream of becoming a teacher to raise me, my brother, and my sister.

The impact of losing my Mother didn't really sink in until I had my third child in 2008. Of course, I grieved when she died, but it wasn't until I needed a Mom because I was now a Mom of three young sons, that it really hit home that she was truly gone. I no longer had someone to vent to about my day-to-day struggles, victories, or humorous happenstances. I no longer had parental knowledge that was just a phone call away.

She was so important in shaping who I eventually became as a person. I often wonder what my Mother would have thought about my decision to become plant-based as a way to mitigate my MS symptoms, or what she would have said to me when she found out that her youngest daughter had Multiple Sclerosis in the first place. What comforting motherly words she would have spoken to me. I know that she would have been over the moon at the fact that I penned a book, as she loved to read, and she had passed on her love of reading to me.

It took me a few years to realize I still do have a mother.....my mother-in-law.

I started calling her Mama P, because somehow "Mom" just felt wrong. It stuck. You always hear about the proverbial Mother-in-law....but I won the in-law lottery with this one. I did still have a Mom.....she just didn't birth me. She has been a constant source of patience, support and understanding. I don't know what I would have done without her in my life. So thank you, Mama P.

So now I have three children, a full time job with an opposite shift from my husband, all the stress that comes with that, AND a poor diet.

That's it.... keep stacking the deck against yourself Nick.

After my third son was born, I can remember getting many strange sensations that were not because of working out, or lifting something heavy at work. I was feeding my youngest son in his highchair one day, and the pinky on my right hand started to twitch as I held the spoon. I remember thinking...that's odd, but I didn't really put too much stock into it. That's when the symptoms really started to stack up, and I could no longer ignore or explain away my body's warning signs. I had taken a turn on the road of illness and disease was my final destination.

Cheese, I know....but the description seems to fit.

One of my most alarming symptoms happened when I was lying in bed one night. I had insomnia in those days....another wonderful way to build disease.

I wanted to sleep, but it just wouldn't happen. It eluded me because I could feel a strange sensation...pins and needles all the way up and down the right side of my body. It was annoying because I was trying to sleep, but at the same time mildly unnerving.

"What would cause that!?" I thought. My body was lighting off emergency flares, and I had my blinders on. So, what does my body do to get my attention? It ups the ante, and fucks with something I simply cannot ignore.

My vision.

Remember me talking about this most concerning symptom at the beginning of my book?

Since sight is a pretty important sense, I don't mind telling you, I was scared shitless. Now, mind you, I wasn't blind, but it dramatically changed the way I saw colours, and realness of objects. We never really know how much we take advantage of something we come to depend on because we don't think about it. It's like breathing. I liken it to going from HD-TV to the older TVs where you turned the knob to a particularly bad channel and there was a lot of fuzz or snow. (I'm showing my age here, the younger folk will probably have no idea what I'm talking about.)

I could only discern obvious shapes...there was no clarity or definition. I would also get bright spots in my central vision that would only diminish if I looked at something peripherally. Anything I looked at straight on, such as text, became impossible to read, because there was a big ball of snowy light where my central vision used to be. This condition still affects me today in my right eye......(Google credit: Central vision is the most important part of a person's vision. It is used to read, drive, and see pictures or faces. Good central vision allows a person to see shapes, colors, and details clearly and sharply. An area of the retina called the macula, which is the lining at the back of the eye, provides central vision.)

Now, I have always heard that sudden vision changes are bad, (that's one of the first symptoms of a stroke, isn't it?), so needless to say my body had gotten my attention with this one. *Well played body. Well played.*

◊ ◊ ◊ ◊ ◊
A K Q J 10

This set off a chain of events that I remember well. I've never had so many doctors' appointments in such rapid succession before.....and I had epilepsy as a child, so I am used to doctors. The first was with my General Practitioner. I'm sure that after he did the standard tests when I described my symptoms, there were alarm bells going off in his head. I then saw an Optometrist, who put me through another battery of tests, and who I'm sure heard those same bells my GP heard after viewing my eye tests. He then referred me to an Ophthalmologist, who then referred me to a Neurologist. Gauging from the number of people the Ophthalmologist had in her waiting room, which looked to me like a casting for Pirates of the Caribbean......... It was a sobering reminder that this was some serious shit.

Then came that fateful day in September of 2013 when I had the follow-up appointment with my doctor. I went into his office and sat down to receive the most devastating news I had ever gotten in my life. I had just been given the diagnosis of MS.

I didn't respond the way my doctor expected. I don't think. I think I was in shock. I didn't cry. I didn't exclaim..."Oh, Woe is me!!!" I even remember him being slightly annoyed because instead of crying, or throwing my hands up in despair... I asked him about a rash I had on my wrist.

He was probably thinking..."I just gave you this devastating diagnosis, and you're worried about a rough patch on your wrist?!!"

To be honest, I wasn't sure what that really meant in the grand scheme of things but I remembered that that's what Richard Pryor (a comedian from my generation) had, and that he was wheelchair bound towards the end of his life, and died at an early age.

I remember going home and telling my husband, and crying and hugging him.

Wow....I had MS.

Now it was starting to sink in. My life would never be the same.

How can this be? I'm a mom of three young sons. 40-years old. (Little did I know at the time it was sometimes referred to as "The Mom Disease," because of how it commonly strikes during childbearing years. Women are four times more likely to be afflicted than men. That's another little factoid I came to know.......it commonly strikes smack-dab in the middle of a woman's fertile years, and symptoms often improve when pregnant and spike after birthing a child. That would explain my heightened symptoms after I gave birth to my third son.

Now....I somehow had to break the news to my three young sons.

At the time they were 10, 8, and 5. So when they came home from school the day I got the news, I sat them all down at the kitchen table and told them their Mom had something to tell them that was pretty serious.

Now, when you're a little kid, you tend to think the worst thing that can happen to you is that you don't get picked first for the soccer team, or that you might do something embarrassing at the upcoming sleepover you've been invited to.

I told them I had been told by my doctor that I had something called Multiple Sclerosis. I went on to explain the little bit I knew of the disease (which wasn't much, to be honest), and I could see the dawning realization, especially in my oldest son's eyes, that this wasn't your average parental talk. This was a game changer. One of the first questions they had for me was... *"Are you going to die?"* With tears in my eyes I went on to explain that this wasn't going to change things much, (or at least, I hoped not)..... that I was still the same Mom, and that I would still be there to cook them dinner and tuck them in at night.

My oldest realized the seriousness of the situation more so than his brothers, and went off by himself. After my two youngest went about doing their after-school routine, I set out to find my oldest son to talk a little more in-depth about how it was going to affect things. I found him sitting cross-legged on the floor in the back room with the pocket door closed. I slid open the pocket door and sat down to talk with him. The tears in his eyes just got my waterworks flowing again, but I tried to explain to him that I was going to do everything in my power to fight it and not let it impact his life, or mine too much hopefully. (I continue to fight this shit disease with everything I have.) I told him that people can live a fairly normal life with all the advances in medicine and the different treatments they have for the disease now. After all, it's 2013 not 1975......it's got to be better right?

I remember my son Nolan, my middle one, coming up to me the morning after I told them that I had MS. He told me he had had a bad dream. In his dream he was going to a nursing home, because that's where I lived, and he wanted to see me. He walked through the front double doors. I was sitting to the left in a wheelchair but he didn't recognize me. I was all wrinkly and old.. (apparently in his young mind this is what MS did to you). This upset him so much, and he was bawling as he was recounting his dream. Truth be told, so was I....In his dream, he started to walk past me, because he didn't recognize me and I called out to him..."Nolan...Nolan..." When he saw how decrepit I was, he started to cry...and he woke up crying. He came and recounted the dream while it was still fresh in his mind.

That was tough to deal with. How do you tell your kids everything's going to be fine, when you don't know if it will be?

After things settled back to our normal routine over the next couple of months, I decided that I didn't want to take my relative good health for granted. I had always wanted to see the East Coast of Canada.....so by golly, we were going. To my financial advisor's chagrin, I pulled out most of my RRSPs so we could book a 30hr train trip to Halifax. I didn't know how much quality time I had left in life thanks to my diagnosis, so I wanted to live for the NOW.

Now you might think....30hrs....on a train??? And I get it. My MIL thought the same thing. We had never been on a train for that long, so we got the whole works, sleeper cars and all! It was one of the BEST experiences we've ever had. That began my love affair with the East Coast of Canada. It was such an amazing vacation. One for the books. My kids loved it so much, that after we got back home my oldest was incredibly sad to find that he had awoken in his own bed instead of in the hotel room in Halifax. I was so glad that we were able to take them on a vacation that they absolutely loved.

We went to Prince Edward Island (PEI) the very next year. We had purchased property there after we got back from Halifax, as it was a place we always wanted to visit.

That's the year I fell in love with the smallest province in Canada......Prince Edward Island.

That started an almost unconscious obsession with someday retiring there. While there on vacation in 2015, I found the Forks over Knives Cookbook at one of the stores in the mall. We had watched the documentary prior to going on our trip, so we were aware of the benefits of Plant Based eating. (I didn't let that stop me from having a final vacation pig-out!)

All the way on our drive home, I read it, and got more and more excited with the idea of changing our diet. I picked out recipes and made a grocery list. But I was still faced with a hard decision. How to go about treatment of my fateful diagnosis? Should I take medicine or not? Should I see a Naturopath or???......to be honest, I didn't even really know what kind of doctor treated what I had.

I struggled with the idea of taking medication, because from everything I had been told, for MS, the only medication available for treatment at the time was in injectable form. I would have to inject myself every day with a needle. Ugh. I was not a huge fan of needles to begin with.... I was instructed by the nurse who came to my home to show me how to properly give myself a needle, that I should inject it in a different spot every time because the medicine killed fat cells upon injection, so I would end up with tiny indentations in my skin, kind of like cellulite.

That was not a pleasant thought to me and steered me more towards natural solutions. Also the fact that with some medications, you only need to take an injection once every 5 or 6 months boggles my mind. How does it help you if you take it that infrequently, or another question...how can it POSSIBLY help you if you take it that infrequently? I didn't want medicine floating around in my body for 6 months...no thanks. That also begged the question in my own mind, how can a medicine that kills fat cells upon injection be good for you? Your body is made up of cells isn't it? And if it kills fat cells, what's it doing to my regular cells?! I remember receiving a call from our local pharmacy regarding the prescription that I had placed at my Neurologist's urgence. I was told by my neurologist that there is no proven natural method to slow or stop the disease. But, let's be honest, I was on the fence about taking medication anyway. I've seen the commercials........the side effects seemed worse than the actual disease itself.

 But it wasn't until my pharmacy called me, that I made up my mind once and for all surrounding the question of whether or not to take the standard pharmacological medication.

The pharmacist that called to fill my prescription informed me that while I was taking the medication, I may want to consider wearing a mask in public and that I might also want to steer clear of touching my eyes, nose, and mouth. That boggled my mind because I didn't need to wear a mask up until that point, or worry about rubbing my eyes, or picking my nose. (I'm being facetious, I don't really pick my nose......) I was trying to wrap my head around why I would voluntarily inject myself with something that forced me to wear a mask on the daily, or to become a germaphobe because it lowered my immune function. *Begging your pardon, but that seemed ass backwards.*

While I was struggling with exactly how to treat my new diagnosis, my husband was searching for natural ways to combat it, as he knew I was on the fence about the medication. He came across a doctor named Dr. Swank, who treated MS with some degree of success solely with diet in the 1940s.

Food as medicine?!

Well, that's the only encouragement I needed... I love to eat! I proceeded to get a hold of his book (which was hard to obtain because it was out of print, but I managed to get a used copy off the internet). That started my path forward into attempting to treat my disease with food, and little else.

Once I received his book, I read it cover to cover. I decided that although Dr. Swank had a proven diet to help control MS, it wasn't necessarily very healthy by today's standards. (Who the hell am I eh?!) Dr. Swank allowed meat and cheese, mayonnaise and butter and other high fat, animal based foods that I now know to be unhealthy. His diet limited the amount of fat that one could have in a day, but the foods that were allowed were by no means healthy, at least in my opinion. From everything I researched about diet, meat and more so dairy was horrible for you. The more I looked into diet as a possible way to at least control MS, the stricter I became with myself. Plant-based seemed even healthier. After watching a few documentaries on the merits of plant-based eating, we decided that based on the evidence, that that, was the lifestyle we were after, and since I was the only cook in the house, that pretty much decided it.

We were changing our diet.

My husband said he didn't care what he ate as long as he didn't have to cook it. Fair enough. Cooking wasn't his forte....building and fixing was. So that is pretty much when we decided we were going plant-based. Both my General Practitioner and Neurologist were against me treating my MS with diet alone.

They said there is no evidence to suggest it works, and that the medication currently available was a far smarter bet. I just didn't know and couldn't picture how my body could heal while simultaneously rallying against the medication and its toxicity. (Because let's face it...the standard medication is not great for the liver....)

So, I went plant-based without medication against my doctors wishes......But, I don't know if any of you have picked up on this...I'm a fairly stubborn, bull-headed kind of gal, and once I get my mind wrapped around something, it's hard to unwind it.

It became a family affair. We got the kids involved by having them pick recipes they wanted to try out of the plant-based cookbooks that we were quickly accruing. We wanted them to have some choice in this big change we were making to our lives. I had people ask me all the time if my children were plant-based too! Well, unless they were undercover covert child cooking prodigies that I was unaware of, they pretty much ate what I cooked.

I even encouraged them to try cooking them on their own......with supervision of course!

After we got back from our trip to PEI, I was eating very healthfully. Plant-based and minimally processed.

I experienced no symptoms of MS.

My skin, which had been acne prone my whole life, and that didn't clear no matter what product I tried, was suddenly clear and radiant. I'm not tooting my own horn, that's just what people told me all the time. At the same time, it's amazing the number of people that have an opinion when you tell them that you do not eat meat.

Then came the questions.... Are your kids vegan?? (Like they had a choice!)........Don't you feel weak all the time? What do you eat? And every vegan's personal favourite: Where do you get your protein? This went on for about three years. Every lunch hour at work was like an interrogation session in some bad television crime drama. I don't know why people feel it's ok to put your diet down just because you choose to leave meat off of your plate. My children were doing wonderfully, excelling at sports because of their increased stamina......and my husband dropped so much weight so fast, people were wondering if he had the big "C." We all felt wonderful all the time.

I decided that food interested me so much as a way to heal, that I went back to school for Nutrition and got my certification as a Registered Holistic Nutritionist, or RHN. After a few years of eating extremely healthy, I began to take my relatively good health for granted. Isn't that always the way?

My work became more demanding so I started preparing more and more quick, processed plant-based meals, and we started eating more and more plant-based fast food. Crap food is crap food, it doesn't matter if it's made from plants or not.

Needless to say my health began to be affected because of the way I was choosing to feed my body. It seems with MS, there is always a part of your body affected more so than the rest. At least it was that way in my experience.

My legs were my affected body part. It was subtle at first, a little limp..... a slower, more unsure gait. From 2018 to 2021, my legs and more so my balance was how MS played out its song in my body. (Not a melody I enjoyed)

I was forced to go off work in 2021. The job I had held for 29 years, I could no longer do. I fell several times at work, and was relegated to light duty work more times than I care to count due to my inability to stand and perform the job. My employer didn't want me there anymore because I was a liability. They even went so far as to have people watch me to ensure I was not putting myself in the path of inherent danger, thereby putting their bottom line at risk.

Looking back, I now know that they broke a number of rules regarding privacy and disabled rights. Eventually it got to the point where I had to go off on short term disability because I was having too much trouble navigating the workplace. Short term turned into long term. One day when my husband came home from work and we started discussing a retirement party for a lady we both had worked with for years. She was moving to a city up North.

The housing market where we lived was BOOMING and people were getting triple the amount that they originally paid for their home. There was never a better time to sell! The house that we had purchased 16 years before and had raised our kids in, was not doing me any favours anymore. It was a ranch style home in the country with nothing but farm fields around. I was declining fast not only due to my diet, but because there was absolutely no challenge for me....I was living in a ranch-style, rural home. If you don't use it, you lose it was a saying that I had heard many times in regards to my disease. It is very true.

I was also quickly sliding into depression, and did not even realize it. Partially because our house was in the country, making it hard to stay stimulated when by myself and partially because there was nothing for me to do while home by myself all day. I never wanted to go anywhere, or do anything, and I welcomed sleep. It was my favourite time of day. I could no longer even cook for my family or grocery shop and run errands. That was a big one. I could no longer physically do for my family. I could not stand at my counter for any length of time. Cooking was one of my favourite things to do, and an important way that I showed my love and affection to my family. There was a guilt that went with the realization that I could no longer provide for my family in that way, that was hard to escape. I guess it would feel the same for a man who couldn't financially provide for his family. Providing is a thing of pride, and important to a man. I'm the Mom, I'm supposed to make dinners, pack lunches, and generally supply my kids with what they need for the day. I could no longer do those things.

This definitely had an affect on my mental well-being.

My husband noticed my mood changes (how could he not, I wasn't exactly easy to live with) and suggested I join an online MS group, so that I had people I could talk to that shared my struggles. People I could turn to and talk to when I was feeling low, who knew EXACTLY what I was going through, because they were going through the same challenges. I joined many an online MS group, but by far my favourite is the group tied to David Lyons and my OptimalBody membership.

Here's a little blurb, if you'll indulge me, of a very important person in my journey, and the reason for my ever-lasting hope in how I can improve myself everyday............

David Lyons, co-founder of the MS Fitness Challenge (MSFC) with wife Kendra, has dedicated his life to helping people with MS understand and be educated on the importance of fitness in their lives. He has been a trainer and a trainer educator for more than 45 years, working with people from all levels of fitness and with many diverse goals. His specialty is the community of people with challenges, whether physically limited or dealing with the progression of aging as a baby boomer.

Lyons is a recipient of the National MS Society Milestone Award and the faith based author of David's Goliath, a book on his journey to a body building stage with MS.

He is also a speaker/writer for the Fellowship of Christian Athletes, a former writer of

Everyday Health, which reached 50 million visitors monthly, and the owner of the OPTIMALBODY fitness brand, which features his Training Program and RBS4 Home Gym System.

In 2013 David received the Health Advocate of the Year Award with Lou Ferrigno. In 2015, at almost 57 years old, he was the only person with MS to receive the Health Advocate Lifetime Achievement Award from Arnold Schwarzenegger, as well as the Lifetime Fitness Inspiration Award in Feb 2016 at the Global Bodybuilding Organization's International Fitness Expo.

In January 2017, David received the Special Recognition Award from the National Fitness Hall of Fame, and later in the year, he was honored as a Founding Partner of the organization's Institute for Learning.

David is considered the face of fitness for those who have challenges worldwide and his fitness book, Everyday Health & Fitness with Multiple Sclerosis was a #1New Release on Amazon while both his MS Fitness Training Specialist and Ms Fitness Specialist certifications partnered with National Federation of Professional Trainers (NFPT), MedFit Education, ISSA and other fitness organizations, educate trainers internationally on how to work with MS clients. David is also the Vice President of Adaptive Sports for the United Intercontinental Bodybuilding Fitness Federation (UIBFF).

Lyons is a 2019 inductee in the National Fitness Hall of Fame for his work as a fitness educator and he has appeared on Good Morning LA, Fox News, CBS, NBC and other news outlets.

He was literally staying ahead of the disease by exercising. But not just exercising, exercising in a very specific way.

Not just going to the gym and lifting weights. Brain to muscle connection is very important for people with neurological diseases, and he knew how to help repair/preserve that. He tweaked and developed his program, and then started a Facebook group that I am a member of to this day. It is my daily zen.....I love to work out now thanks to the results and improvements I've seen by following his program. His knowledge of how to work within the body's limitations, and then progress past those limitations through thoughtful, specific exercises, that are done in a very specific way for people with any sort of limitation, is amazing. He has won many an award, and I encourage anyone who is struggling with this shitty disease to look him up.

I have heard a thousand times while looking into plant based eating and healthy alternatives that the body WANTS to heal....we just have to supply it with the right stuff. Now while I was going through a nutritional epiphany if you will, my husband was not very happy at work, and constantly felt unfulfilled. One day my husband came home from work, grumbling about his mundane job and jokingly said something about moving to PEI. Of course, this was just one positive of many in favour of making the move. Hmmm.....it doesn't take much to get my cogs turning.

There had never been a better time to sell. We could sell our home for a higher price, pay off our bills, and still have enough left to purchase a home in PEI outright and live mortgage free in a place we always want to vacation in.

I'd also heard that the schools on the East Coast were excellent. Well, that set the plan in motion and we began looking for houses in my favourite province. We soon found a house, and put in an offer. We took advantage of the market, sold our home, (in a record breaking 10 hours, and for our exact asking price!) and purchased a house out east.

Wow.

For months after we sold, I could not believe that this was the turn my life was taking. We had lived in this house for 16 years, and had raised our kids in it, but we could not pass up this opportunity!

We convinced my Mother-in-law to move with us, because we couldn't picture living 24 hours away from her, and the next thing you know she had put her place up for sale as well. After only a few weeks, she had accepted an offer, and had her place sold. She had put money down on a lease for a perfect abode out east! Things were moving now….we were actually moving to a new province!

It's hard to picture when you live in the same area for almost 50 years of your life!

I could not believe we were doing it! We rented big 53-foot trailers and moved our things and cars across the country. I had a bit of experience with renting trucks and arranging drivers in my time at my previous work, so it was easy to set up.

We literally got out right as the housing market in our area started to turn. We had snuck through the window before it could close!! (Much like my teen years….). Two weeks after my Mother-in-law sold her home, the housing market started to fall. Talk about timing!! As you can imagine, it was an adjustment for our children, but they all quickly settled into the east coast life, made friends, got jobs, and started attending their new schools.

Kids are nothing if not resilient.

Our realtor out east gave us the name of a carpenter because we needed to have some work done on the home we had purchased out there. Once we "landed" on the island, we met with him and began to go over the plans for our house. Since we purchased a house out east while living in another province, we pretty much bought the house sight unseen, so as you can imagine, there were some things to be done.

It was a 3-bedroom, 1-bathroom saltbox home from the 20's....

Doing the math...we quickly figured that there were not enough bedrooms. We wanted to ensure the kids all had their own rooms. For the first time ever. (Now we would see who the real culprit was when it came to a messy room!)

My MS had gotten so bad that just walking around my ranch home back in Ontario had been a problem. Having an "accident" while trying to get to the bathroom 10 ft. away became commonplace. I did a lot of laundry. Wouldn't you know the home we purchased sight unseen only had an upstairs washroom? Oh no.

When we first moved in, I literally thought I was going to have to purchase a portable toilet and do my business in what would become our pantry! It would have been the only private place to set up my makeshift shitter on the main floor.

I could not imagine moving my bowels on a portable toilet in a pantry surrounded by crackers, canned goods, and cereal. Classy. How undignified. I would also have been mortified to have my husband of 20 years be forced to empty my toilet pan upstairs. That decided it for me. Since necessity is the mother of invention, I quietly vowed to myself that I would try going upstairs to do my business.

Having lived in a ranch style home for the past 16 years, I was not sure how I was going to fare with the 14 steps I had to go up when nature called. Or, if I would be able to make it without an accident, or without falling down them to my death. (visions of my husband finding me in a crumpled heap at the bottom of the stairs was very real at this point). But not only was I making it to the washroom, up all those stairs (most times) but the bonus was climbing those stairs was improving the strength of my kegel muscles, thereby increasing my body's own ability to hold my bladder! When God closes a door he opens a window…am I right?

Now, I'm not going to lie, there were times when I didn't make it to the washroom but those times were getting few and far between. It's amazing what the body can do when it is put in a position of need. I was so proud of my body for overcoming this seemingly insurmountable obstacle. But as I mentioned earlier, our new house only had three bedrooms upstairs, so it's kind of ironic that we were now planning an addition that would give us a main floor bedroom and bathroom.

Again.

Difference is this time I can choose to go upstairs if I want. I was almost starting to feel normal again. I was even starting to venture out of the house without wearing a Tena pad.

I preferred to say Tena pad over diaper.

But that is essentially what you're wearing……there's no way around it. But that had improved too! I was going for small drives without one, using the bathroom if we went to a restaurant and choosing not to wear one when I visited my mother-in-law..... and that was huge! She also had a main floor bathroom at her home, and only lived minutes away... so there were really no excuses.

As I write this I am gratefully feeling the effects of my medical marijuana, and I feel like I was meant to write this book.

That everything has built up to this point, and all the things that have happened thus far in my life were meant to happen. The people that have come in and out of my life, however fleetingly, were put in my path for a reason.

I was meant to get MS.

I am actually thankful that I developed the disease. Sounds crazy, eh? MS turned me on to things that I would not normally have given a second thought.... things that are important in life. It has forced me to look at what real health means, and how to get it. Not only how to get it, but that it is possible....and I deserve it!! We all deserve to live a life full of life! Without this diagnosis, I would have stayed in my old life, and would have been a factory worker until I retired, likely getting more and more disabled because there was no real challenge and no real knowledge of what the body needs. We would have lost all the equity in our home and likely stayed in debt.

Now I have a deep understanding of what true health really is, and I am living my best life in the place that I love, and always longed to be. I look forward to the day when I can walk without having to take someone's arm, use my poles, my cane, or my walker. And it will happen, I am sure of it. This is where I am supposed to be in my life, and I am just thankful that I was paying attention to the message my body was sending!

~

Mind Over Matter........

One of the biggest challenges of this disease is staying positive when you're having a bad day.

For me, medical marijuana was crucial to my being able to put things in a positive light. Even when I was struggling just to go up the stairs by literally having to crawl up them because my leg strength was crap that day, or I couldn't bend my knee......when my medical marijuana took effect...I just didn't care. So for me, marijuana was integral to how I dealt with my disease on a day to day basis. (I speak more to this in my Self-care chapter)

Even though I had dark days, I would always try and look for the silver lining. My silver lining was that I had no pain. Yeah, my legs didn't work that well and my balance was for shit but I had NO pain. ZERO. That's a big one. It is hard to have pain and yet stay positive. I've thrown out my back, and the pain is no joke. I cannot imagine pain being my constant companion. I know people who have this disease and that is one of their symptoms. My heart breaks for them. It would be like hell on earth.

For people who don't know me, you cannot tell I have anything wrong with me just by looking at me.... Especially if I was standing still or sitting down. I will never forget being in line at Costco in the height of Covid.

During that time they would only let so many people in the store at a time due to distancing restrictions. So, shortly after they opened, a line would begin forming, and go all the way around the building most times. I usually brought one of my children with me to help me shop. Not so much because of my gimpy ol' self, but because I had three teenage boys....and they ate. A LOT. So I usually needed two carts to hold all the things that I would purchase. My son would push a cart also. This particular day, I'm in line with my son waiting for the doors to open, when the line ahead of us began to move. My legs are the issue but I'm usually okay if I am holding on to something. Hence the cart. But the moment I start to walk, even with the cart, my irregular gait becomes apparent.

You could clearly tell that I had a disability.

As my son was walking beside me, he was simultaneously looking behind me, and he noticed this gentleman (he doesn't really deserve that title) making a hurry-it-up motion with his hands.

Hurry the fuck up.

That's what it said. That's the rudeness of humankind. You have to allow for people like that. Let it roll off your back. If I had a dollar for every time someone offended me because of my disability, I'd be pretty wealthy....

Another example of people's ignorance usually happened when we would go anyplace public, like a restaurant, and I would always be holding my husband's arm, but I don't look demure or like the weaker sex who is accepting a chivalrous escort to my seat.

I look like an inebriated lush taking my husband's arm for balance. You could clearly tell I had something wrong with me physically. You would not believe the stares I would get.

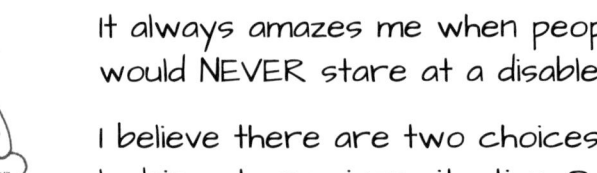

It always amazes me when people stare. I would NEVER stare at a disabled person.

I believe there are two choices when looking at any given situation....Positivity and negativity. I believe the energy that you put out into the world eventually comes back to you, and that both positive and negative things build upon one another like a snowball picking up snow as it rolls downhill.

I truly believe that and have seen it in action in my own life. I believe that I am generally a positive person. I think I tend to look at things primarily in a positive light. Most times.

After my MS diagnosis, I could have given up, listened to my doctor's opinions that there was nothing I could do but eventually become crippled by this disease, taken the prescribed medication with all its glorious side effects, and probably started on the path toward inevitable decline. Not because I took the medication, but because I would have never sought out an alternative solution or learned anything about nutrition and lasting health by going back to school. I would have continued to eat a horrible diet that provided my body with nothing.

(Side note: Nolan's girlfriend almost made me cry today. She told him she's so impressed with me......that I'm a very positive, upbeat person, in spite of my disability. So sweet. The fact that that came across to her in the few times I've met her made me well up with tears.)

But again, you have to stay positive even in the face of adversity......

I owe it all to hope.

If you hope for nothing, you strive for nothing. And to me, that would have been the saddest thing of all.

My symptoms had been exacerbated because there was NO nutrition in the way I used to eat. How is the body supposed to heal itself when you do not give it the right tools to do the job??

Now I am definitely not saying that you should not take your prescribed medication. That was just not the path I wanted for myself. But everyone has to educate themselves and make the decision for themselves based on all the information for their given situation. One can heal while taking medicine. Sometimes it is needed in order to save our life. But, at the same time, we should arm our positive quiver with gratitude arrows and be thankful for all that we have. That positivity will get us through the toughest times. Not the negativity. The negativity will leave us high and dry, and offer no hope. We need hope in the same way we need to look forward to a positive event in our future. Like opening Christmas presents, or lunch with long lost friend we haven't seen since high school. Our body does not heal in negativity. Cortisol runs through our system when we're stressed and gives way to inflammation. When there are always fight or flight situations, our body does not have a chance to return to homeostasis.

We always have to try and think positive to give our body the best chance of beginning the healing process. Gratitude is so important. It is a form of positivity, and it really makes you take stock of your life and all that you should be thankful for. As my Grandma always said, "there is always someone worse off, so be grateful."

She lived to be 94, so I think that attitude served her well.

When I had my first son, I had insomnia for a spell. It wasn't until I watched my Mother die of lung cancer that it really put it into perspective for me. So what if I only got an hour or two sleep, I was alive. Nothing in my life could be worse than seeing the woman who gave birth to me, who raised me, who kissed my boo boo's, and who protected me from the wrongs of life....struggle to suck in air to breathe. Nothing would ever be worse than that....Okay.....Except for losing one of my own children. OK. That would be worse......but losing a parent is up there on the stress scale....

So, when I went to sleep the night after my mother's death, I thought of my mother taking her last breath, and I was no longer plagued by insomnia. Now I usually fall asleep within 10 minutes of shutting my eyes. And if I don't, I don't. I don't sweat it. Big deal, I'll just take a nap the next day. (I take frequent impromptu naps as part of my daily self-care. If I'm tired, I just close my eyes and off I go. That's another thing I'm grateful for. I'm fortunate that I have that autonomy, as not everyone does. My Mother worked herself to the bone....until she no longer could. My children are older, and I no longer work outside the home. Naps are heaven.)

As I stated at the beginning of the book, I am also thankful for my MS. Without it, my life would look totally different today. I think we would have lost our house in Ontario, as we  were living paycheck to paycheck, and with the increase in the interest rates, there would have been no money to make up the difference. Instead, I am thankful that we made the most of the high interest rates, sold our home at a huge profit, and moved to PEI, becoming mortgage free.

I am thankful that I was off on disability. It afforded me a little security knowing that I have steady income coming in, so it bought us enough time for my husband to look for a job in our new province. At least I knew all the bills were covered so we wouldn't lose our shirts.

We might not be able to eat, but at least I knew we had a roof over our heads. There is always something to be thankful for. If you're thankful, you're more positive minded. If you're more positive minded, you open the door for healing.

You can't wait until life isn't hard anymore before you decide to be happy 😉

- Nightbirde

One day you will tell your story of how you overcame what you went through and it will be someone else's survival guide.

- Brene Brown

Strength doesn't come from what you can do, it comes from overcoming the things you once thought you couldn't.

— Rikki Rodgers

Nick's Journal Notes

Ok, I'm not going to sugarcoatt stuff. What you'll read in these notes will be the unfiltered, raw view of MS and how it has impacted my life thus far.

I feel like an x-rated Judy Bloom. I swear and lose my shit quickly, but I try to keep it real. This is where I will highlight my thoughts of positivity and negativity, and show that it is possible to be a glass half-full kind of person even with disease. We'll have bad days, but they do not need to be what we focus on. This journal is to encourage others who struggle with the everyday. Keep working at it. Embarrassing and downright undignified, at times, but the point is, one can get through it and come out on the other side.

MS doesn't define you.

(I am including a copy of my daily journaling template I use at the end of my notes here. This is a way you can keep yourself accountable everyday. Go get em' friends.)

December 14th, 2022:

Today was another first. My legs felt extremely good today. I went with my youngest son to the grocery store. I drove, which is a little challenging for me, as I have to get in my Jeep. It is easier for me to get in the passenger side as there is no steering wheel in my way. When I get in on the driver's side, I have less space to get my body in, and I have to maneuver my legs under the steering wheel, so it's a little more challenging.

So, I crushed that, I got in myself. I drove to the grocery store, and parked by the cart corral. I had already pre-warned my youngest that I wanted to try getting a cart by myself. So we got out, and I proceeded to get a cart. As we're walking in the store, Emerson kept praising me for how great I was doing, and how proud he was of me for testing myself like this. He will never know how much that meant to me. So we stopped for what we went for, and I kept asking him if he wanted a "treat" for helping me, like some tangerines or grapes...he then explained to me that he doesn't need a treat to help his Mom. That he was only too happy to help. Awwwww......We got back home and I got out and got myself into the house.

Win.

Today my MS seemed like the smallest part of me, and I haven't felt that way in a very long time.

Never give up.

Feb,27th,2023:

Today, like a couple of times in the recent past, my disease seemed the smallest part of me.

I worked out, cooked for hours in the kitchen, and swept the floor. Then Jason came home and asked if I wanted to go check out some material for our shack. I was pleasantly surprised that the place we were going had carts....not to mention, numerous places to rest. I checked out the item my husband wanted my opinion on. I put the cart back and walked back to the jeep, with my handy-dandy poles, and got myself in. Felt great, and I didn't wear any "protection" in public either, which is a win by itself. All of these little wins are adding up to big wins and my disease is taking a back burner. Screw you MS!!

March 13th, 2023:

Today was a huge day for me. Today is my rest day from working out.....which lately for me has been a bummer, because I enjoy my workouts so much! I never used to enjoy working out, but because I'm seeing some progress in my mobility, I am more motivated to work on myself. That is huge. It's hard when you put in the work, and you don't see any results. It's like eating nothing but salad day after day, and not losing weight! But today, I really noticed a difference in my "outside of the house mobility." That is where my trouble usually lies. Outside. The ground is more uneven, and unpredictable. I had a dentist appointment today. Not only was I getting around the dentist's office a little easier, but I got there by myself. I still used my poles, but I didn't have to use my husband's arm. I felt a little more assured, a little more balanced. I was more autonomous. That is huge. That is the one thing you lose when you become disabled. Autonomy. I know it may be too much info for some, but I didn't wear any protection today, and I was able to hold my bladder. I have more control over when I go. It is a public space, with people other than family around, so if I have an accident....I would be mortified. I felt normal for the first time in a long time. This is to encourage those who struggle with the everyday. Keep working at it....

March, 16th, 2023:

Today was another awesome day! I went to the bank by myself, and stood in line to speak to a teller. I also went to the grocery store by myself. I parked near the cart corral, so I could walk in with a cart. I only purchased a few things, and then schlepped myself back out to the car. I picked up my sons from school, drove my son to work, did dishes, and made dinner. I haven't been this autonomous in almost 3 years! A great, great day! Don't give up...you can always improve...even when you think it's hopeless. I'm not running marathons mind you, my movements might be slow to some, but who cares?! My doctors all said I was headed for inevitable decline, and there was no solution, other than the standard medication. Well, I'm working off of just diet and exercise....I love proving my doctor's wrong about that.

April 22nd, 2023:

Sometimes I get down on myself, because if I don't make leaps and bounds, I feel like nothing is happening. What you don't see is that minute improvement that may get you to that leap or bound.

Right now, I am sitting in the pedicure chair getting my feet pampered. And you know what? I drove here by myself. Got into the building by myself. Got up in the pedicure chair by myself.

This is the second time in as many months that I am doing something entirely on my own. It is such a feeling of freedom that you do not understand until you lose it. I have gone to the grocery store, and now to the nail salon completely alone.

I'm grateful and positive for where I'm at and where I'm going…my future is brighter than it has been in a long time.

Don't get down on yourself if you don't see a big improvement right away……you are making minute changes that you notice over time!

July 31st, 2023:

No workout today.

Terrible day for balance…fell today, hit my head. Just a poopy day. A red day as I call it. Here's hoping tomorrow's a better day.

Aug. 18th, 2023:

When is this shit going to get better? So tired of giving it my all, only to be shit on symptom-wise. Started my morning by doing my exercises, then I made pico de gallo. I stood at the butcher block and chopped stuff for it. Legs got weak so fast! I haven't had a good day all week!

Aug. 19th, 2023:

Well, today was a decent day until.....I went out to our shack....I coloured.... I love colouring. It's so relaxing. Then, on the way back to the house, Em asked me if I was okay as he was bringing some dishes in the house. I felt strong, so I said yes. But as I was walking back to the house, I used my poles. Until I got to the car. Then I began to use the car for balance. All of a sudden my hand slips off the car and down I go! I got into a fight with the concrete of my driveway and lost.

Fuck, that hurt....I cut up my lip, smashed my front tooth something horrible, sending me new realms of pain....and scratched and bent my glasses! The worst part though, Em came out just as I went down. I hate when my children see me fall.

Aug.24th, 2023:

Went to a nice restaurant with a patio today. We got a nice shady spot under a tree. Then, I got a bit chilly in the shade, so we decided to move to the sun. After sitting for 45 minutes with the sun beating down on me, I went to get up, and discovered I couldn't. Even with Jason and Em helping me I couldn't stand.

The worst part is the stares that you get from people. I had this sweet, elderly lady ask if I needed help...but honestly....if my strong husband and young son can't lift me, what are you going to do? I finally managed to get up and gimped to the stairs, where I had to sit again. The car was too far away to walk. Not for anyone else, but for gimp girl it was too far. So, I sat there until the parking spot directly in front of me was free, and my husband backed into it, and then they both helped me to the car.

It was a horrible experience. People staring, and no doubt, wondering if I may have had one too many glasses of wine. So, I was finally able to get my ass in the car. The latter part of the evening turned out better.

Aug 25th, 2023:

Colouring in the shack, feeling better....no falls today.

Aug 28th 2023:

MS is such a mixed bag. You never know what you're going to get! My legs don't feel fantastic, but I've gotten a lot accomplished!

Did wash

Did dishes 4 times

Folded clothes

Cut and roasted cauliflower

Made rice

Smoked tofu

Worked out

Did challenge

Made big salad to last the week

Went upstairs to bathroom many times

Wrote in book

Made dressing

Made salad to eat

Aug, 29th 2023:

Felt ok all day. My oldest came over. Walking into the living room from kitchen, I fell.

Again, I hate it when my kids see me fall. I'm Mom. I am supposed to be a pillar of strength.

Sept, 9th 2023:

Passed out today and pissed myself. Nice.

Sept. 19th, 2023,

Woke at 1am to go pee. Couldn't get out of bed, and sit myself up. Ended up sliding on the floor because my legs wouldn't bend. Fuck. All I wanted to do was go to the bathroom. At least I didn't piss myself.

Oct. 14th, 2023,

It's 10 pm, and as I'm going to bed, I realize my balance feels better, and my legs a little stronger. I try to practice standing on one leg, and walking to the bathroom without holding on to the walls. I hate WASTING my legs feeling good by going to bed. I wish they felt like this during the day.

Oct. 25th, 2023,

Peed the bed last night. Damn, it's been a while since I've done that. Shit. That sucks. Good thing we have a mattress protector on our bed. Silver lining: I was due to change my sheets anyway, and it gives me an excuse to finally put on the mattress topper I got Jason for his birthday. Always looking for the positive.....but I've said it before, I'll say it again...this disease is very degrading. I've been very weak this week, and my balance has been for shit. At least I haven't fallen in a while. That's good. Again. There's that silver lining.

Oct. 27th, 2023.

Peed the bed again last night, and I know why.....maybe I'm trying to re-capture my youth.....hee hee....no...I know why....I woke up and I had to pee, but I didn't want to get out of my warm, cozy bed, so I held it and drifted back to sleep. While I slept my bladder relaxed and released it's contents. No more, I don't care if It's -40 outside the covers, I'm getting up to pee. Beats changing the bed, or trying to hide it from my husband because I'm embarrased.

Nov 1st, 2023,

Well, I took my mood enhancer, and I'm very positive this morn. I finished my workout, and did the monthly challenge. Here's what I posted:

Can only improve from here! After I was done doing the challenge, I thought I would take advantage of the fact I was already on the floor and do a few stretches! So I did some back and hip stretches. I am going to try and do it after the challenge each day...I'm on the floor anyway.......who knows, by the end maybe I'll be stronger and more flexible!

Nov, 2nd, 2023,

It was frustratingly hilarious this morn, as I went to get out of bed to go to the washroom. I could not get my left leg out of the sheets. I couldn't bend it enough to pull it free, and I did not have enough abs strength to sit up and physically free my left foot from the covers. It was like a comedy show. No one knows the little things that happen every day with this shitty disease!

Nov 10th, 2023,

The day started with a simple trip to Walmart. Simple enough eh?..... I have never had a more frustrating shopping experience in my life. My legs didn't feel too bad, so as my husband and I entered the store, I went my way to get what I had to get, and he went his way to get what he had to get. I'm usually ok if I have a cart. It acts as a "pseudo"-person...... I shopped for the produce I needed. o.k...doing good..... Then I needed to walk all the way to the pharmacy for various sundries. I couldn't find what I needed, so I walked all the way to the other end of the store where the cash registers are located to ask a cashier where I might find the item I was looking for.. She told me what I was looking for was back in the exact spot I had just come from! Anticipating the Himalayan trek I had before me, I thought I'd better rest my legs. So, I erroneously decided to lean against one of the center displays to take the weight off my legs and rest. That was a mistake. When I did, the center display that I was leaning on.........slid. The next thing I knew I was on the floor. I have to say this particular Walmart wins no awards for rushing to the aid of the lady who has fallen and can't get up.

Spasticity is a strange thing. It's like your affected muscle is a taunt, stretched rubber band. I'm sure I looked like quite the spectacle as I tried unsuccessfully to bend my uncooperative left leg. This went on, in my mind anyway, for what seemed like 10 minutes. Which is a long time to be prone on the floor of a public place, in my humble opinion. Finally one of the more astute Walmart employees asked me if I needed help up. After the nice employee picked my fat ass up off the floor, and I explained to the nervous looking staff the reason I was on the floor in the first place, I then saw my husband come up the aisle. I'm glad he wasn't there to see the spill. There is just something about the man that you're intimate with seeing you sprawled on the floor of a Walmart. Ok, I'm up.

Now, the mental calculator in my head must have been on the fritz this particular day along with my balance, because I thought that the money that I had in my account was sufficient to cover the cost of the various things I had gathered........I was wrong, by about $50.

I had the money, but in another account. Matters none when there are people in line, and you can see that they don't truly buy the story of how it's just in a different account.

I didn't think it too big a deal and I told my husband as much, and I started the process of transferring my money. That was when the trouble with my phone started....... . A few months back I must have gotten a virus on my phone, as apps and pages would just randomly open on their own... I had zero control over it. It's like it was possessed or something. It seemed to clear itself up, and I had no more trouble with it.....until now. What should have been a simple trip to Walmart, turned into an embarrassing event. My husband cares more about what people think than I do, so he was getting visibly upset at this point. . We ended up just putting the $50 overage aside, and paying for the rest. Miraculously the phone demon had left when I got in the car, and I was able to transfer the money. My husband must looked the fool as he went back inside to pay for the items we had left behind just moments earlier......... In the end, we got everything that we went to Walmart for in the first place, so it ended well at least.

Nov 14th, 2023,

Going off my current way of eating until main floor bathroom is done. Because if I'm not getting my water in for the day, its almost as if I'm cheating......I should have a certain amount of water......so it's almost like........."what's the point of being so cognizant of your food if you are not getting the water you should be drinking everyday? It is more of a permission if anything............ We were out enjoying family time in our new shack. All of a sudden I get the urge to pee. I told Jason I had to go to the washroom, and that there was a distinct possibility that I may shit myself. Our addition which was to include a nice new bathroom wasn't done yet.....so I had to walk across to the house, walk through the house and all the way upstairs to the washroom up 14 steps. If I was able to hold it, it would be a miracle.........lady luck was on my side, and I made it. Thank God for small favours. Thank you for sparing me the indignity of soiling myself……whew…….

December 8th, 23:

Fighting a cold. Almost hacked up a lung this morning. Fell twice today, I dropped almost everything I picked up! I was wondering why I seemed extra uncoordinated this morning. That's when I learned about "pseudo-exacerbation." Aaaah… that explains it…. (Description of pseudo-exacerbation in self talk/self-care.)

Dec, 31st, 23

I have to try and drink more water. Feeling great! Legs feel better than they have in months!! Feel more co-ordinated, better balance. Going to really try and stick to this way of eating for 1 year. Salad with healthy dressing and minimal cooked food. Discovered a new thing that helps me control cravings….my liquid gold sprinkled with nooch! I am not sure what is lacking in my diet that makes me crave that, but it is healing, so bring it on!! (recipe for liquid gold in misc. section)

Jan 5th, 24:

Well, I got a virus, not sure what it was, but it literally PARALYZED me. I could not walk, or toilet myself. It was horrible. I had to bring my walker up from the basement, so my husband could use it almost like a wheelchair. He was literally my nurse maid for about 4 days! I think that if my situation was like that all the time, I would opt out of this life. That is how I felt as I was lying in bed unable to move. Not to say that is how you should deal with a situation like that, but it is how I truly felt. If I ever get to the point where I couldn't feed, toilet or generally care for myself………I'm out.

I will not put my family through the burden of being my nurse-maid……(Now, don't get me wrong………I am not promoting this as a course of action in the least………but that is just how I felt in the moment.) I continue to be thankful every day that my body rallied and made a comeback……

Jan 22nd,24

I've been back on plan (healthy eating) for a while, starting to feel stronger.

Everything feels so surreal, so intense….like I am actually in the moment. It's really weird. I can't describe it.

Jan 28,24:

Man I'm tired of this shit. We're getting renos, so we're kind of living in chaos. The fridge is super far from this sink right now, as is my preparation area. So I'm having to gimp across the room to prepare food. Something as simple as adding olives to my salad becomes a major chore. I have to get them out of the fridge, get them to the sink to drain, and then gimp back to my butcher block all the way across the kitchen to put them in my salad. I've almost fallen several times while I'm doing this. Life is hard. Then my husband walks in and asks why I'm in such a bad mood. I wish I had the power to put others in my place so they could feel what I feel and deal with my stupid problems. I feel so alone sometimes.

Ahhh….suck it up Nick. You're still fairly mobile. You have no pain, and you can still pretty much do for yourself.

I have to take a step back sometimes, and realize all that I have.

Feb,18,24:

Feeling great today. Well………better than I have in a long time. Happy, been watching and applying the secret. Recommitting to WFPB diet. Hopefully it helps.

Feb,19th,24:

Got up at 5am. Legs felt wonderful. Balance much improved. Trying to remember to feel grateful and happy.

Feb, 25th,24:

Went away for weekend with hubby to Moncton. We got a cheap motel room……you know the ones….where you just park infront of your room…..the access is not through a large lobby, but right there….in front of your car. I love that. I hold onto the car until I reach the room....I don't have to gimp through a lobby with my poles or my walker. So happy to be out of the dust bowl that is our house right now. I was SO happy all weekend to be away from the stressors of renovations and all the tiny fights that seem to erupt between family members because you're all on edge from living in a constant state of construction. I know it is a first world problem, as I am getting my house renovated so what am I complaining about, but it is stressful to live in chaos and clutter. Since I was happy my legs were pretty good. I was still eating plant-based, but I didn't worry about fat content or whether it was whole foods.......I just ordered off the menu and enjoyed it. It made me feel normal.....like I don't have a disease where I need to be super vigilant about diet and drink.

We went to Costco. It was nice to get out and socialize with people. I need that, I am a social person. I used my walker. It was nice to shop and look around at a store and I had a seat when my legs got tired. Before I moved, I used to be embarrassed to take my walker out to stores because I grew up there, so I didn't want to run into anyone I knew. Who gives a shit? Funny what you place importance on in your life eh? This was a Costco I had never been to before, so I didn't care what I looked like to people. It also allowed Jason some autonomy as he was able to go off by himself, and he didn't have to worry that I would face-plant.

There is something to be said for being happy and not stressing. I didn't fall or piss myself all weekend. That's a win. Live life, be happy.

March 28th, 24:

This disease sure does make you feel alone. I'm sitting on my couch, staring out the window. Just me and my dog. It hurts me deeply when people plan things and don't even consider I might be interested in partaking. Don't even ask me if I would mind getting out of the house. I know why too.....I am an inconvenience. I'm slow and I take too long to get around. Exact reason why I wanted a dog. They NEVER make you feel alone.

April 3rd, 24:

Today is my middle son's 18th birthday. I posted a little memory lane movie on Facebook. He has a great head on his shoulders and knows what he wants out of life. That's all that you can hope for. House is almost done. Just waiting on kitchen. I cleaned the backroom floors. Jason swept and mopped the main house floors. They look so much better. Feeling very fortunate and blessed.

Did my daily OB challenge. 10 controlled reps.......felt great! Took my "medicine"......... While I was relaxing,, I thought of the idea of adding my marijuana portion to the book.

April 5th, 24:

Positive note today. Went to pick something up in Summerside. It's about 45 minutes-1 hour away from us. I had to pee while we were on the road. We stopped at a gas station. I made it all the way to the washroom (at the back of the building) by myself. Peed, and actually pooped twice......and not in my pants......so that's positive. I love that It's been almost 1 year since having to wear a TENA pad when going out anyplace public.

I think I accidently double dosed with my medical marijuana today. I am TOO high. I like that it's not deadly though.........if I happen to intake too much, I just chill out and let it pass.

April, 6th, 24:

Positive day today! Feel good......it is my rest day.....and I'm meeting with my friend Sukriti in a couple days! Wow. What a turn my life is taking....

April 8th, 24:

Sent a text to my brother today. I haven't talked to him much since my father passed last year. I feel for him. He has tried to make amends for the stuff that happened in our childhood. It is not his fault. He was a child too. His reactions to certain things in our past was totally understandable. I just let him know I was thinking about him, and that I love him.

April 9th, 24:

10 years ago, I never would have envisioned the life I have now. That I'd be 50lbs lighter, much healthier, and living

smack dab in the middle of Charlottetown, PEI in my newly renovated home......

That my husband would be a gardener at a cool, trendy art gallery on the island......

Or that I would be going to a local coffee house to meet with my editor friend about a book I'm writing......

Wow....I am feeling very positive and grateful.

I met with Sukriti, my editor friend today. I was amazed at the connection I felt with her. She felt like an old friend. My biggest fear in meeting her would be that I would do something embarrassing, like piss myself, or faceplant ... .but I did neither......so it was a good day.

April 11th, 24:

UGH. I awoke at 5:38am to the sound of my dog retching. No one will ever understand the frustration of not being able to tell my legs to move and have them NOT listen. Silver lining: At least he jumped off the bed before getting sick. Thank God.

April 26th, 24:

I had a small emotional epiphany thing happen this morning. I was sitting with Em, and we were talking about my reading at the writer's guild, and how I couldn't believe I might be going to the next one by myself.

By myself......I have to let that sink in a little bit.

April 28th, 24:

Sent to Sukriti after our little get-together at my house......

"I was so excited for today....I didn't fall asleep until 3am....

Thank you so much for coming, and lovin' on Murph....

I am so glad you ate too much....my Mom would be so proud that she raised her daughter right...

'Never let them leave hungry', she would say.....

It was so nice meeting Chantel......she is a sweetheart.

Maybe I'll finally be able to keep a plant alive for once!

Sukriti had come over, and brought Chantel......her friend......who I met for the first time. A beautiful person......and she brought me a little plant when she came....

May 1st, 24:

Today Em brought down his guitar and showed me a few songs he has been noodling around with.

Blown away. Blown away.

He has no idea the love I have for him, or how proud and honoured I was that he chose to share that with me.......at 16.

He also has a killer voice.....although he doesn't think so....... Like father like son.

May 2nd, 24:

Today was a day packed with positivity, and physical and emotional exhaustion.......but in a good way.

Firstly, thanks to Chantel's (my new friend) patience and kind heart, I walked down my street.......down the street to the crossroad at the top of the street. Might not seem far to most, but to someone with a disability.......that is like trekking the South Pole. In a day. Without any sled dogs....and no shoes.

Ok, maybe not that bad....but hard.

So we got to the bus stop.....I rested... (I literally haven't been on a bus in 35 years.) Got off the bus, walked with Chantel to the corner, walked across the street, through a park. I went to a rally at a legislative building on PEI!!!

It was my first rally ever.

I listened to a lady (Rene) I became acquainted with, speak eloquently to the legislature on a topic that I hadn't realized was a problem. Or even given much thought to. Banning trapping and snaring. Some poor lady on the Island lost her dog because someone planted a snare on her property without her knowledge......terrible.

I made it without an accident for 4 hours while we were there. Then we went for coffee at The Gallery. We walked.

We were there for 3 hours. The lady who spoke before the legislature drove me home. I put my body through things today I have not done in MANY years.

May 7th, 24:

As I am furniture surfing around my house and I realized I am like a functional 80 year old. I can get around slowly, but everything tires me out….and I have to take frequent breaks. I have to hold on to walls and furniture to get around because my balance is for shit. But even though I'm like an old person mobility-wise……..I'm still kicking ass and taking names today.

I've:

Done dishes 4x

Cleaned kitchen sink

Made fudge

Did OptimalBody Challenge

Grilled Pitas

Folded wash

Took out summer clothes

Put away winter clothes

Smoked tofu

Took the stains out of 4 shirts

May 11th, 24:

Happy Birthday Grama!

I got out and about today. It felt nice. I went to the bank with Nolan. The people at the bank were so kind They saw me gimp in with my poles and they insisted I go first. There was like 9 people in line! People can be so nice sometimes...it was the same way when I was pregnant. I told Nolan to stick with me if he wanted to be first in line.......I'd hook him up!

May 13th, 24:

Feeling blessed.   Rockin' out to a little "Release" while cleaning my beautiful kitchen at 9:05 am on a Monday. Stark contrast to what I was doing 10 years ago at 9:05 on a Monday.

Reach for what you want.

May 17th, 2024:

I have to start driving more. I noticed that I'm getting more trepidatous because I never go out of the house anymore, let alone drive. I feel like a Hermit.

May 22nd, 24:

Sometimes you just have to see the hilarity of this disease. Today I struggled to crush a cereal box with my foot. Probably a common everyday thing you do before throwing it in the recycle. You step on a box to minimize it, so you can fit more in the recycling. I crushed it, but then my foot got stuck in the indentation I had created, and I didn't have enough strength or ability to lift my foot out of the well I made, so I comically ended up dragging it around the floor like some recyclable snowshoe!! UGH!! Then a little later the same day I struggled to pick up a simple bread tie that had fallen on the floor with my spastic fingers before my knees buckled. This disease is fun stuff!!

May 30th, 2024:

Happy Birthday Mom......

Missed the wall today on my way to the bathroom. Since my balance is non-existent these days, I have to furniture surf and grab walls. A good recipe for an accident. Anyways, my hand slipped and down I went, on my ass. I fell on the concrete floor in our new addition. At least I didn't smash my head. (That is one of my fears...that, and falling down the stairs and paralyzing myself. It took me about 25 minutes to get off the floor...another day packed with fun stuff because of this disease.

June 18th, 24:

A couple weeks ago, I was going to feed Murf his breakfast and I was walking across the kitchen (not holding onto anything mind you....) when in his excitement, he proceeds to run right in front of me....tripping me. I wish I could have seen it in slow motion from a third person view, when I went down. His food I was carrying became a kibble fountain, and it went EVERYWHERE. (If I wouldn't have been so hurt, it would have been comical I'm sure.) Now I have to furniture surf and grab walls wherever I go because I hurt my back when I fell.

I am in bed...and I'm thinking my legs have never felt heavier. I have to get a plan together for my health moving forward!! This is ridiculous.....I am a RHN for Christ' sakes. I KNOW how to eat healthy. I don't know why I have such trouble eating cleanly. You'd think not being able to move around normally would be motivation enough! Food is SO powerful. I guess when you have no control over your situation, it becomes almost a drug. My goal today is to try and get all water in, and to eat as cleanly as I can....*get with the fucking program Nic...*

July 3rd, 24:

Well, I will be 51 in 5 more days. 51. Wow. Where does the time go? Thanks to Murph, I have been furniture surfing ever since he tripped me. I have to get back to the strength I had last year.

Aug. 22nd, 24:

Our friends came down for vacation last week and stayed in the shack. It was so nice to have them. Great memories made. I am feeling so blessed and fortunate. I feel like 'The Secret' is happening in real time. Most things I have wanted for my life are coming to fruition.

I think of my mom and I know she would be proud of me. Even I am amazed and astounded by my newly discovered skill.....writing. Enjoying the ride, but trying to take it all in.

Aug, 23rd, 24:

I would love a maid!!!

I lost my balance CLEANING today. I didn't hurt myself (I usually don't thank goodness.) But I took like 20 minutes trying my damnedest just to get off the floor. Last year I could do downward dog and get myself up, but this time, Em had to come down and get my fat ass off the floor! I have to get back to my strength of last year. Strength with MS is a fleeting thing and can come and go depending on what's going on in life. I know I can, because I was worse before, and I got stronger.....it's a matter of time, determination and focus with me. When we moved in 2022, I was using a walker. My walker has been in the basement since late 2022......but, that's if you're not counting my tango with paralyzation at the beginning of the year.

I am going to be a little stricter with my diet, make sure I'm getting my water intake as well as ensuring I am following David Lyons workouts and challenges to the best of my ability! (Like this morn, I woke at 3 am and did my tris and bis!)

My MSFC family has been integral to my mental and physical health. The encouragement and support I get from them is amazing. They have seen me through some of my darkest days. I also have been writing on the MSFC platform, having my articles published, and having a blast!

Jan, 6th, 2025:

I have not written in here for a bit.

Called my brother for his birthday today. We chatted for a bit.

I had my friends for colouring in the shack on the weekend, it was so nice to have some estrogen around, as I live with 4 men...and even the dog is male!! We just chatted, ate and coloured! It was so nice. I want it to be a monthly thing. I am trying to convince myself to venture out on my own a little more now that I have a car. I hope to go to Writer's Guild at the end of the month by myself. Lord, I am getting scared to drive by myself and be out without help.....that just means I should do it more. Just be safe and bring my phone.

I am trying to get a little stronger, as I found out a lady I used to talk to in my MS group, passed away in May. I talked to her often, and she often expressed her concern over declining with MS, but she was such a fighter. I was saddened to hear of her passing. Rest well, my friend.

It is just starting to hit home to me a little bit, as several of the ladies that I used to talk with daily, have either passed, or are not doing so well. This disease is so horrible. It robs you of your autonomy and dignity. I will never stop trying to rally against this shit disease. Every time I don't feel like giving it my all, I will think of the fallen heroes I have known with this disease, and do it for them.

Jan, 10th, 25:

The Chinese Calendar said 2025 for the Ox (which I am) was going to be a good year. I feel like I'm living 'The Secret' in real time!

Jan, 29th, 25:

I am re-investing in my health...Going to try to...

-get my water in

-push myself in my daily workouts and challenges to my limit.

-do 5 min of tai chi every day.

-eat MOSTLY coleslaw

-think more positively

-touch my husband affectionately in some way.

I have gotten away from using my template, but I'm going to start using it again to make myself more accountable.

For stress relief...cook, workout, take your weed, play with the dog.

Feb, 3rd. 25:

One for the books today. As I was going into my kitchen, I was holding on to my counter...when my hand slipped. Fortunately, the 500lb butcher block was there to break my fall. the only problem was, I broke the fall with my face. It felt like I had been given a left hook by Mike tyson! No joke. I thought I had busted my eye socket for sure.

Jason bore witness to my spill...thank God he did...I kept going over in my mind how this little scenario would have played out, had I been alone. It made me think that it wouldn't be such a bad idea to have those little emergency call buttons to wear on your neck...like the old lady in the "I've fallen and I can't get up" commercials of the 80's...

I knew by how upset my husband was that it was bad...

Call the ambulance bad.

there was blood all over the place. (I found out from the ambulance attendants that there are lots of blood vessels in the face...so it bleeds pretty profusely when cut)

My two sons could hear in their father's exclamation of "OH MY GOD, NICK!" that it wasn't because he was sampling one of my delectable kitchen creations, so they came running down.

My oldest would make an excellent paramedic. He was so gentle and soothing. Telling me to just lie still and that everything would be O.K.

he filled a big measuring cup with warm water, got a cloth, and proceed to clean up th bloody mess that was his mother.

Emerson kept asking if I was okay, all while keeping a respectable distance. The ambulance attendants arrived..very quickly as they had just left a call a few streets over. They got me up, and in a chair. They asked how it happened, and went through their normal routine, putting that little clothespin on my finger that measures heart rate and taking my blood pressure, which was great according to one of the attendants. Good to know...a tleast I wouldn't die of a heart attack.

I knew they were asking me questions to test the state of my mental acuity after such a dramatic fall. They were asking things like my dog's name and my old address, as I was relaying a story where I fell and split my ear open in our previous house. 21 stitches...

After assessing me, they determined it did not warrant an ambulance ride to the hospital. They packed up and left.

After the excitement died down, and the adrenaline wore off, my husband bandaged the gash on my forehead. I took it easy for the next couple days, relishing the relaxation. No cooking. No cleaning. No dishes.

My doting husband was now my nurse-maid. I don't want to have to break my face everytime I want this kind of treatment......but a girl could sure get used to this...

My Daily Template

I have found having a daily outlet to write down how our day has gone - good, bad, or ugly is very important. We have to be accountable to ourselves. Honesty is the first step towards recovery. One can include the things that are important to us. If you colour code it, you will see a visual representation of how you're feeling as the days stack up, and whether or not you're improving, or stuck in a rut and you need to change something. In compiling my notes for this section, I would mark my days as follows:

Green- Good day
Orange- Okay day
Red- bad/hard day

Here is the day-by-day template I use for journaling.

- DATE: (This is what I colour green, orange or red.)
- Food:
- Water intake:
- Sleep:
- Self-care:
- Attitude:
- Legs:

- Flax oil
  (the components in this oil actually comprise our cell walls- but it can only be used as a salad dressing as heat damages it's properties. Oh, and it's expensive as fuck.)
- Workout:
- Medication:
- Bowels:
- Trips to the bathroom: (The most I've ever gone is 21x in one day!)
- Things done today:

If you hope for nothing, you strive for nothing.

- Nicole Tracey

Sometimes you never know the value of a moment until it becomes a memory.
- Dr. Suess

Happiness will never come to those who fail to appreciate what they already have

- Buddhist Teaching

Self-care and Self-talk

Here's where we get technical, and I delve into the scientific side of MS.

This is a more of a clinical chapter and it is meant to explain how it may affect you......so here goes..

MS stands for Multiple Sclerosis. It is a condition in which the body's immune system attacks the protective covering of the nerve cells in the brain, optic nerve and/or spinal cord, called the myelin sheath. (Always makes me think of a Lord of the Rings term for a sword covering...."Gandalf....don't forget the ancient Myelin Sheath....we need it to protect Frodo!!!")

Demyelination may lead to a loss of sensation or feeling in whatever area of the body corresponds with the damaged area of the brain, optic nerve, or spinal cord. It's like there is a giant eraser erasing different spots in your brain, or on your spine, causing you disability in said area. There are lots of symptoms that MS can cause, but not everyone will experience all of them.

Each person's experience is unique. My eyes were my first real indicator something was wrong. Thus far, MS has affected my balance and my ability to walk unaided.

Symptoms of MS may include but are not limited to:

Fatigue: I find sometimes changing venues (bed to couch) helps me to fall asleep if I happen to not be able to sleep in my bed.

*Numbness and tingling

*Loss of balance and dizziness

*Stiffness and spasms

*Tremor/pain - have experienced tremor, but NO pain. Thank Goodness!

*Bladder problems

*Bowel problems

*Optic Neuritis

*Problems with memory and thinking

These are the symptoms I am dealing with because of this disease.

Since we're speaking of symptoms, I wanted to mention something called *"pseudo-exacerbation."* I have had it happen to me a couple of times, and it's something to be careful of. Google Credit: Unlike a relapse that causes new symptoms, existing symptoms are exacerbated due to this phenomenon but will return to normal once the cold or illness has passed and internal temperature has dropped. (Just be sure to be extra careful if you're feeling under the weather, as you can be more prone to accidents and falls.)

One also has to make room for self-care.

Self-care means quite literally, caring for our whole self. That can include anything we do to look after our physical, spiritual, and emotional health. Holistically. Self-care helps you maintain healthy relationships. That in turn allows us a better relationship with ourselves. Engaging in a self-care routine has been clinically proven to reduce and/or eliminate anxiety and depression, reduce stress, improve concentration, minimize frustration, diminish anger, and also increase happiness and improve memory.

Self Care is more than just putting our feet up at the end of a long day.

There is **physical** self-care, which simply means taking care of our body by feeding it well, ensuring we're getting enough sleep, engaging in physical activity, and tending to our physical needs by way of appointments, taking our prescribed medication and generally managing our health. I do this by choosing to eat a whole food plant based diet, drinking sufficient water and performing my daily exercises specific to my disease.

Psychological self-care entails the way we think and the things we choose to mentally put our focus on. They play an important role in our mental well-being. This involves doing things that help us to stay mentally healthy. Inner dialogue and the way we talk to ourselves is important for robust mental health. Be positive with yourself. I am a glass half full kind of person. When looking at any situation, I tend to see more positive than negative. I try not to let the little things bother me.

Spiritual self-care does not necessarily mean we have to be a religious person. It does not necessarily have to involve religion. But if that is important to you, it can. It also can include anything that helps us nurture a deeper sense of meaning, understanding, or connection with the world around us and the universe as a whole. It may mean different things to different people, and can be achieved through thoughtful meditation, or enjoying a religious service. I would classify myself as agnostic, meaning I believe in something grander than us, but I have no idea what it is.

Emotional self-care is important for being able to deal with our emotions by including some healthy coping skills in our self-care repertoire. Activities that may help us to express our deepest feelings and emotions. This could simply entail having a friend or partner you confide in, or expressing your thoughts through journaling. I am a huge advocate for writing out your emotions.

When we practice self-care, we produce positive feelings, thereby boosting motivation and self-esteem, leaving us with increased energy with which to support ourselves and our loved ones.

There are many self-care practices that help ensure that we stay in a positive frame of mind while going through our healing journey. Whatever gives you true joy.

They are many but are not limited to:

- Reading positive affirmations
- Listen to or watch a comedy
- Write the things you're grateful for that day
- Take a nice bath
- Breathe deeply in a quiet place with your eyes closed
- Light some candles
- Exercise - proven to release endorphins
- Close your eyes and breathe deep
- Walk in nature
- Buy yourself flowers
- Write a list of things you'd like to do
- Journaling
- Make a vision board

- Declutter a room
- Read a personal growth book
- Listen to your favourite music
- Watch a comedy
- Plan a getaway
- Colouring in your favourite colouring book
- Cook your favourite meal
- Spend some time with friends
- Go out for date night
- Try something new
- Give yourself a manicure
- Call or text someone you love
- Do some yoga poses
- Listen to your favourite podcast
- Spend time with someone who inspires you
- Stretch
- Do a spa day
- Do a digital detox
- Eat a salad or drink a smoothie
- Go out in the sunshine
- Visit your favourite place
- Get a massage
- Hug someone
- Drink a glass of water
- Get dressed up and put on some makeup
- Sleep
- Watch the sunrise/sunset
- Diffuse essential oils
- Do something nice for someone
- Go out for a coffee
- Read a book
- Try something new

Self-talk is the way we talk to ourselves, or some call it that inner voice. I talk to myself ALL the time. Out loud too. Self-talk can affect our mental health as well as impact your relationship with others. Negative self-talk can actually make it harder to deal with chronic pain. It can also affect how you view yourself. Replacing negative thoughts with positive thoughts is sometimes hard but necessary to get out of the rut one may be in, and begin the healing.

Positive self-talk can improve self-esteem, the way we handle stress and overall well-being. It may also help to reduce any symptoms of depression and anxiety. It can soften the way we see ourselves in terms of positive body image, allows us to feel more in control of our life, can help with chronic pain, motivate, and help to calm us down.

Surrounding ourself with optimistic people and practicing positive self-talk every day is an important component for happiness.

Visualizing positive situations that we want to achieve is an important component in self-care. For example, I want to jog on the boardwalk. I want to walk on the Confederation Trail. I want to walk on the beach and feel the sand beneath my toes. I will feel my feet hitting the wood of the boardwalk, feel the muscles in my legs working, feeling my core supporting my balance. I will feel the gravel beneath my shoes on the Confederation Trail. I will smell the trees that line it. I will walk on the beach with my children again. I will feel the sand between my toes, and I will feel the ocean breeze on my face, and the water lapping at my feet. I will try visualizing these things daily. Find a quiet place, close my eyes and put myself there. Feel. Smell. See it. Happening in our mind's eye. It is important to allow ourselves to think of it as reality. Because then only we will begin to move towards those goals.

If you have MS, you understand that *"if you don't use it, you lose it."*

You must always exercise and move your whole body....or you will lose the ability to. There is no progress without struggle. It is the things that are difficult, that allow us to progress through our limitations. Always push yourself. Safely of course.

The THC Taboo

This little section in Self-Care is dedicated to using marijuana as ACTUAL medicine, its effects on me personally, but also tearing down some of the stereotypes surrounding its use. I have noticed those stereotypes even within my own family. Sometimes my kids, or even my husband will be surprised when I partake in my medical marijuana first thing in the morning. They are thinking of it like I'm just getting high....but it is my MEDICINE!!! The THC specifically helps my neuroplasticity and my mental well-being (which is SO important when you have a disease that causes more depression than cancer!)

So the **HIGH** is what helps me....

This section, so I don't get sued by someone, is all about MY opinions regarding this still-vilified plant. I am not promoting it, or telling anyone they should use it to treat their specific condition. It is all about how marijuana affects me personally, and my own experience with it.

O.K......, I'm not going to lie. I love marijuana. It makes me:

Happy

Positive

Hopeful

More motivated

Less spastic

More imaginative

More creative (allows me to think outside the box)

More focused on the moment (which is great for David's workouts....but in no way does he promote it; I'm just stating that as my personal opinion.... it helps me focus on the muscle movement)

But as with any medicine, I had to learn to respect the fact that I am using it like medicine and not abuse it, or intentionally overdose for the euphoric effects. Because let's face it.... when you have a disease like this......it's so hard to stay positive. If I intake too much (which I have done unintentionally on occasion I can expect to experience negative symptoms such as:

Dry mouth

Getting lost in a loop of my own thoughts

Feeling cold/chilly

Muscle tension in neck

Over-analyzing the moment

Shaky hands

Increased temporary memory loss

But I would rather have these side effects than the ones that are caused by conventional medicine any day of the week and twice on Sunday.

(REDDIT credit......The origin of the statement above harkens back to 1746. The South Carolina Gazette printed that church was holding service once every day (twice on Sunday.)

And…..that phrase was also used in the early 1900's when professional wrestling was more of a carney act in a circus…they'd have a show every day of the week, and since Sunday was a day of rest they would have two shorter fifteen minute shows.)

*created note in phone called Forget Me Not's which helps me remember things I may have temporarily misplaced in my memory banks due to my recent marijuana use.

Downside…..you have to remember to write it in there. ☺

One of the major stereotypes surrounding marijuana is that it causes you to be unmotivated. Lackadaisical.

One of the reasons I love it is because it has the exact opposite effect on me….it actually increases my motivation. Not only does it increase my motivation, it increases my neuroplasticity, making me more apt to do the things I'm motivated to do without injury. I experience increased range of motion, improved balance, more thoughtful movement when getting up to do a task. It also increases my desire to work out. It's natural. It is regulated by the government. (Not sure if that's a positive or a negative…no… it's a positive for sure, as I know because it's government regulated, I'm not getting back alley weed laced with fentanyl.) Plus, because it's labelled as medicinal, which, for me it absolutely is......I can claim it towards my healthcare.

Although, I must say, I recently looked at the ingredients list of some of my favourite marijuana beverages......It made me think.....why are there so many chemicals in marijuana drinks? You don't find that in most beers...in beer, you have natural ingredients like grains, hops, yeast, and water. I don't give a shit what colour my beverage is. The drink I chose today had FC #1 Yellow and Brilliant Blue... Why would they put known carcinogens in something that may be used to fight cancer?! Hmmm...makes you wonder.....

I still use it like a medicine even though it's a beverage, and I enjoy imbibing. Another thing that I like about marijuana, is that there are so many ways to get the medicine into your body. You can smoke it, bake with it, eat it, and drink it! A doctor once told me that it is impossible to overdose on it. You cannot say that about ANY other medicine.....

I like marijuana because I can dose it myself, and I can control the effects. I adjust the inhalation as my spasticity dictates. I decide based on how I'm feeling at that particular time.

Part of Self-care for me is my use of medical marijuana. Originally I was going to dedicate an entire chapter to this topic. I was going to entitle it "Up in Smoke"......(not sure if there is a copyright infringement there...) I was five pages into the chapter when I proceeded to hit the DO NOT SAVE button, obliterating the 7 hours worth of work I put into it. I was so upset because when you hit do not save it should prompt a "Are you frickin' sure?" question.

I was in a sort of reverie after working so long on the computer......oh well, lesson learned. I have decided to condense it and include it in my self-care chapter, because it really is part of my self-care routine.

The gist of the chapter I was trying to convey was all about the benefits I have experienced with it. I am not in any way promoting it or telling people that they should use it to treat their condition. It was all about my specific experience with it, and how it has helped me on my MS journey. I just wanted to break down some of the stereotypes regarding this still vilified plant. As I stated earlier, I have even noticed my own family displaying some of these stereotypes. Not all people who use medical marijuana are lazy "potheads" who do nothing but lay about eating Doritos and watching t.v. But, you do you.

My munchie go-to's

Just so you're armed with all the tools if you happen to partake of the wacky-tobbacy, I am going to give you a list of the things that I allowed myself when the THC component of my medicine took effect....

Any raw vegetable you want (Dip it in cashew ranch and you're good to go)

Any fruit you want

Natural popcorn drizzled with liquid gold, nutritional yeast, and salt

PB&J on whole grain toast

Salted pretzels and dark chocolate (I try and limit this one, as it's more of a treat)

Loaded coleslaw (as much as you can stuff your face with)

Whole wheat pita with Liquid Gold

Lots of water

Just be a good person. Love who you can, help where you can, give what you can.

- Thoughts Wonder

The pessimist sees difficulty in every opportunity, the optimist sees opportunity in every difficulty.

- Winston Churchill

The 3 C's in life: Choice, Chance, Change. You must make the choice, to take the chance, if you want anything in life to change.

-Zig Ziglar

Give Thanks

I struggled with this section for a long time. Whether to include it or not. Ultimately I included it because I wanted the world to know how integral these people were in my healing journey. Some of you were in my life briefly, some of you folks were my daily lifeline....and some of you fell somewhere in between, peppered along my story. I will be forever grateful to all of you. Here you are, in no particular order.....

Anabelle Oosthuizen

Kristen Luchinskey

Pamela Resch Weitzel

Jo-Anne Farncombe

Kelly O'Connell

Krissy Avila Sallustro

Linda G.

Amber Dorian

Marianne Luz Kane

Mel Hogan

Rhonda Dodson

Shauna F.

Susan Chiakas (deceased)

April Waller

Val B.

Cza Isaac Terry

Tannis Romer

Rachel Miles

David and Kendra Lyons

Angie Gensler

Mama P.

Kelly Skierczynski

Pete Bowlby

Gilbert Steen

Ivon Ramos Webster

Susan Jankura Rowan

Bettie Stousland Kensmoe

Rebecca Roman

Sukriti Chhopra

Chantel Ramanan

Nicole Drew

Stephanie Stevens

Dawn Potter

Derek Nantais

Barry Beutell

Mel Hogan

Shrinivas Krishnamurthy

Julie Erickson

Emily Kammerer

Jennifer Richley

Meera Valencia

Grete Doc

Emilia Bachelier

Beverly Boo Rothstein

Lord Edward

Julie Erickson

Tasos Markos

Lesley Bain

Carrie Russo Wilkens

Chris Chambers

Lucille Popp Allard

Jackie Nagy

Jen Prest

Terrie Sellers Kincheloe

V Brian Gagliardi

Tony Jarrett

Tricia Meloche

Linda Graveline

Jennifer Richley

Lesley Bain

Alma Gonzalez

Lorraine Gallegos

Carolina Japiassu

Gabriel Japiassu

Rafael Japiassu

Lucy Boss Adelaide

Leo Lemire

Alma Gonzalez

Barbara Morin-Leclerc

Noel Flynn

Ivon Ramos Webster

Maureen Pageau

Gerry-Lynn Murphy

Marilyn Phillips

Ray Mccarthy

Jessica and Mike Fritz

Brian Jean

Jessica Tracey and Madison Haskell

Maggie Mariani

Kelly Ann Beaulieu

Sometimes you have to let go of the picture of what you thought life would be like and learn to find joy in the story you are actually living

– Rachel Marie Martin

You create your own
universe as you go along

– Winston Churchill

No one can go back and start a new beginning, but anyone can start today and make a new ending.

—Carl Bard

Continuing the journey...

So here it is a year later, and I continue to fight this monster MS. Except this time I am hopeful for the future and what it holds for me. I have a game plan that is helping me get a little more mobile and active, and to partake in the everyday of life where as I was not before. My walker has been in the basement for the last year or so. My progress might not be visible to some, as I am the only one who is aware of what I've had to overcome. That is the mixed bag you get with MS. You have to stay positive and hopeful, or it gets depressing really quick.

I continue to exercise using David Lyons methods that he developed specifically for MS. Eating whole foods, plant-based, I sometimes feel that I alone am supporting the local cabbage farmers with how much cabbage I consume. I love my loaded coleslaw. It is not easy, and it is a constant battle but one I feel I'm winning.....ever so slowly. But, I allow myself an indiscretion every once in a while.

I created a vision board a couple of years ago, and although I know not everything I wrote down has come to fruition yet, I am hopeful that most things that I have scribed will eventually come to life. I joked with my husband that I will start a Vision Board party trend where you write the things you envision for your life, and then 3-5 years later depending on the timeline you set for yourself, you reveal it to see how many of the things you put down there came true. Invite the people closest to you to the unveiling. Enjoy refreshments and your favourite plant-based food and have a good time. So, if you see this new party trend sweeping the internet... you heard it here first, folks!!!

I couldn't wait....I opened my Vision Board. It's only been three years, and there are things on there starting to come to fruition...my writing a book is a big one, but so far, there are probably 6 or 7 things that I have ticked off my list.

Damn, I should have waited the full 5 years!

My kids have settled into their new province well and are adjusting to their new surroundings. My oldest, Carson, who is now 19, soon to be out of his teens and turning 20 in a few months, has a great job where he has learned several roles. He hosts, is a waiter, and also bartends on occasion. I'm fairly certain that bartending for him was on my vision board. So that's cool. He is my level-headed thinker. My middle son, Nolan, has made many friends here, and is entering his final year of high school. Graduating next year....unbelievable. Smart, tall, and might I say handsome....My youngest is adjusting to life here, scoping out possible career options, teaching himself guitar, and turning into one pretty great human. All of my boys are pretty great humans, but I am a little biased. I am very blessed.

We are still adjusting to our new province as we are still waiting on renovations to our house. It has been over a year since we moved, and although I feel very fortunate that we are mortgage-free and living in beautiful PEI, we have not gotten to enjoy it too much as we have been living basically on the main floor of our house and relegated to sleeping in recliners while we wait for the addition to be built. I know.....first world problems, right?!

I just received a call from our contractor literally minutes ago that a crew is coming to dig in preparation today, and the foundation will be poured tomorrow! That is music to my ears. It has been a long drawn out process, and I am eager to get it over with. I feel very blessed that we are even able to fund this little project (shout out to my mother-in-law also) and customize a beautiful home that we can enjoy for many years to come. Construction is underway!! The hole is dug and foundation poured. Cannot wait to enter the exciting next phase of the construction process!

It is stressful right now, as we basically kicked my oldest out to live with his Grandma, so we could commandeer his bedroom, because without the addition, we are sleeping on our recliners in our living room. We told him it was only temporary, until the renos are done as it just doesn't feel the same without him at home. We are also getting a dog soon.

We rescued him from a euthanasia list in Texas. There is a wonderful group in Texas that adopts dogs out to people in Eastern Canada. They rescue dogs from Texas and Mexico, neuter them, get their shots up to date, and then transport them to people who adopt them in Eastern Canada. We have adopted a Siberian husky/Pit mix. We are going to call him Murphy! He is just a puppy right now, and we are all so excited to get him. Even my husband who has expressed his disdain in the past for getting another dog, is excited!

I find that it always helps to have something to look forward to, whether it be a date night with your spouse at your favourite restaurant, an upcoming concert by your favourite band, or greeting a new furry member of the family!

Recently my father passed away and I went back home for the funeral. It was an awkward feeling for me, as it has been years since I have seen some of my relatives, and the looks of pity were disheartening as I greeted them with walker in hand for the first time. We travelled back home by train, which is a whole different experience when you cannot walk that well. I could not traverse the long concourse that went to the train by walking. So for the first time in my life, I was pushed in a wheelchair!

I got to say it was a nice perk because we were boarded first! I would have given anything to walk it myself, but the train staff was beyond professional and courteous.

I have a new appreciation for people with disabilities now that I have one myself, and I have had to travel with one. I find people look at me more because I am fairly young and walk with my walking sticks or walker. It annoys my husband when people stare at me while I'm trying to maneuver myself around.

Now that the house is underway, we have started making plans with friends to come and stay with us. I am hoping that I may be a little more mobile at that point, as I would like to go to the beach, maybe the national park. I don't just want to sit at home and drink beer because I'm too crippled to go anywhere. I want to partake in life and show our friends and family the island.

It's funny, but I don't know how many times in the recent past I have written about where I hope to be in a couple of months...but then those couple of months come and go and I am not really any further ahead. A little disheartening, but that is where the positivity must kick in to carry us through those negative times. I've included one of my favourite quotes, which I think really applies here.

"Sometimes you have to let go of the picture of what you thought life would be like and learn to find joy in the story you are actually living." ~ Rachel Marie Martin)

I recently fell and smashed my face on my concrete driveway....Remember me telling you about that? I didn't even have time to put out my hands. Smack! Full-on contact with face to concrete! Boy that hurt! Not only did I tore up my lip, I think I jarred my front tooth loose and damaged it. I don't think it's my imagination that it is a little greyer than the other. Well, another injury due to this shitty disease...

When I think about it, I have spent thousands of dollars trying to improve my current situation. I always have these grandiose visions of how I will incorporate these new purchases into my life. My middle son said, instead of me buying things to help my external self, I should spend less money on gadgets, and instead try to work on my attitude. He's not wrong. It does need work.

I swear like a trucker and have a tendency to lose my shit quickly. But I really am more of a positive-minded person and tend to think of the good in a situation first. I just have a quick-to-flare temper. That's the magic that is me..I guess. No, I really should work on myself. We always should strive to better ourselves. I told my son that the reason I spend money on things that I perceive will help my disability is because when you have a disease that limits your ability to be mobile, you will try anything to get your mobility back. It's not like I was born with less mobility...I had it...and then it slowly disappeared.

I've been on both sides of the fence... So I know what it is like to be able-bodied. I miss it.

I catch myself being mesmerized by watching people who can walk without aid, and how easy it is for them to go about those movements. It's amazing because it all boils down to balance. But it really is the foundation for mobility.

You know I noticed that I can never just have a good day from start to finish. It seems, with my disease, there always has to be something that happens that takes the colour out of my rainbow. (Just made that saying up on the fly....pretty good eh?!) It was the weekend, which is nice because I get to spend time with my husband. The day started with us going for a little drive and enjoying the weather with the windows rolled down on the Jeep. It was a beautiful day. Last year we purchased an outbuilding and my husband redid the inside. We call it our shack. We got home and Jason wanted to go out in the shack. It is our little oasis right now, with the house being under renovation, everything is a shitstorm in our house. So we went out to the shack and I was colouring (I have to think of a new term for that as it makes me sound like I'm five......but I LOVE colouring!!) and Jason was watching football. We were both enjoying the relaxation. I stood up to go to the washroom and started walking towards the door. Before I stepped outside, I suddenly felt VERY weak, and mentioned this to my husband. The next thing I know he is calling my name over and over, and I am on my back. I guess I passed out!! Luckily, I had a backpack on, that broke my fall and prevented me from smacking my noggin. That was the first time I passed out in like 30 years!!! Jason was scared to death because he didn't know what was happening, as I just fell straight back with my eyes open. The reason I got up in the first place was to go pee.

I have friends and family coming next year, I want to enjoy the time with them fully by experiencing the island, as Jason and myself have not yet been able to enjoy the beaches, or walk on the trail, or go anyplace that requires real walking to explore, because of this shitty disease. I have fallen quite a bit over the past little while. I WANT THIS SHIT OVER. It has been three solid years since MS has affected my ability to walk without some sort of device.

So we did end up going to pick up Murphy last month, and he is definitely keeping us on our toes as he is about 6 months old. I tell Jason it is akin to him being like a 4 year old, as he doesn't understand instruction and right from wrong yet. We have to teach him all that. The cat is not too impressed with her new roommate and now hides in the basement most days. Which I find sad, because she's a very affectionate cat. My hope is that one day they will get along.

Hey....I hear the sweet sounds of construction coming from the addition. Music to my ears. It is coming along beautifully, and the more that gets done, the luckier and more grateful I feel. The guys that are working on it are incredible. Honest, hard-working, looking out for our wants while ensuring that our budget is kept in mind. I think I am a little infatuated with Steve, our contractor. Not in a sexual way, but because it's a little hypnotising when a man is so knowledgeable and proficient at what he does. Probably speaks to my primal instinct as a female to have my needs met by a man. That's probably why I still find my husband so incredibly attractive after 21 years of marriage, because he's exactly like that. He is self taught that way. Jason is very smart, like he already knows whatever he is attempting, whether it be building something, or fixing something. I have always seen him that way. I am sometimes in awe of him. Everything he does, he does well. No joke. Whereas, I seem to be like Mrs. Butterfingers who's always tripping, dropping stuff, spilling stuff, and doing stuff wrong. I'm the Shemp in the family. Except in the kitchen....in the kitchen, I kick ass.

In my defense, this disease sometimes makes me clumsy, uncoordinated, and shaky. My hands shake, so it is easier for me to drop stuff. Speaking of my hands shaking... I discovered that I can no longer write. My once beautiful penmanship is marred by my constant shaky hands. I used to get compliments all the time for my writing. I even used to write my best friend notes in high school to get out of class because my penmanship looked so adult. When I tried writing some notes on my pad the other night, I was shocked that I could barely read my own writing! Even my typing has suffered. I used to type very proficiently, but now I hit the wrong keys all the time and have to correct my spelling constantly. Mavis Beacon I am not. Collateral damage of MS, I guess. Could be worse, I could have pain.

~

I came to the realization this morning that I have a shopping addiction. And Amazon is my dealer. No joke. I just spent literally $1679 on Amazon without blinking an eye. Now,  mind you, I'm going to sound like an addict here defending myself by saying that all the items I purchase are useful. I am not buying 177 pairs of the same colour slippers or 79 watermelon forks.....although I have bought one of those forks but have yet to use it. They make them look so practical in the commercial! After my crippled ass hauled in the latest and greatest from the front door, I stared down at the pile which now festooned my entryway and immediately knew I had to call Mama P. (My MIL for those of you who were not paying attention to the cast of characters in my little melodrama)

She answered the phone with her normal cheery, upbeat voice. I immediately let her know this was not going to be our usual jovial chat about the weather or the latest adventures of Murphy the Moose. I relayed to her that I thought I had a shopping addiction. I knew with her history of psychology and working with people in that capacity in the Emergency room (and she had seen the gamut I'm sure...) that she would understand. I explained to her, displaying my own psychological prowess, that I think my aberrant spending is due to the fact that my MS makes me feel so out of control and alone, and that it was my way of attempting to control my world.

MS is such a degrading disease....I pissed myself twice yesterday trying to make it up the stairs to the washroom, and I've fallen 3 or 4 times in the past couple of weeks, one time actually producing blood (I cracked my head on the corner of my kitchen wall going down, and it split a long, shallow cut which proceeded to bleed profusely for over an hour, scaring the crap out of my youngest.) What doesn't kill you makes you stronger right? I can walk around my house, usually holding on to walls or furniture surfing, mind you, but the point is I get around. I don't get out much. All I see all day is Forensic Files episodes and my dog Murphy, to see what new concentric shape he can contort himself in with his leash. We are still leash training him, as I don't think he is quite potty trained yet. I don't want him sneaking off and depositing some foulness in a private corner somewhere, which we would probably smell before we would see, so on the leash he stays.

As if he can sense what I am writing, he just took a giant dump on my dining room floor.

Excuse me a moment while I clean that up......

I am also recommitting to whole food plant-based eating. I find that I keep straying from my healthy eating, as I am human, and sometimes my taste buds win out over my willpower. The things that have improved with my condition you don't really notice....like my alopecia and my lichen planus. (Both have cleared up since beginning my stricter way of eating but it is totally my fault because I keep cheating myself and straying from clean eating. I made delicious homemade pizza for my men the other night, and I went to bed thinking that as soon as the kids get on the bus for school in the morning, I'm devouring like 3 pieces!! But alas, I did not.....I want to walk on the beach all the way to the water and swim in the ocean without the aid of a special mat for my walker or poles. I want to walk on the Confederation Trail holding my husband's hand, not for support but for pleasure.

With my background in nutrition, it's hard to believe the body wouldn't respond to the healing foods, and when you think about how your cells respond if given the proper foods, I honestly do not see how eating clean cannot improve my symptoms. 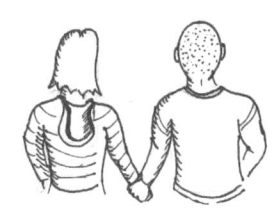 It took 45 years to get sick, so I would imagine it's going to take a while for my body to heal. I have to be patient. I am also going to try and be conscious of thoroughly chewing my food almost until mush. Working in a factory for 29 years with a 16-minute lunch teaches you one thing.......to scarf down your food! I don't want my stomach doing double duty to break down my food because I'm not chewing thoroughly enough. I don't want my energy wasted on digestion when my energy would be better spent on healing.

Keeping my fingers crossed something major improves...like the vision in my right eye. I recently went for an eye exam, and the doctor said if my left eye was like my right eye, I would be unable to drive. It is shocking to me that it is that bad. I guess I am used to it. I can make things out, but cannot read out of it. I guess it's important to be able to read road signs. As I am writing this, I am squinting my left eye shut, to see if I can make out any letters on my computer screen. NOPE. So, anyway, I got sidetracked (one detriment I find with medical marijuana is it deadens my short-term memory. I forget a thought almost as soon as I think of it. It is very frustrating. Samsung notes is my constant companion and my saving grace. If I don't write it down, I will forget it...sometimes it comes back, but sometimes it doesn't. Many of the nights I'm in bed, and sleep eludes me because I keep thinking of ideas for my book or what to make for dinner on my next weekly menu or another necessary Amazon purchase that I desperately require. That's sometimes when my brain does all its thinking. I have to pee and workout now, so I'll be back. I promised myself I wouldn't waste the effects of my medical marijuana by being lazy.

I'm back....we were discussing the reasons why I thought I had a shopping addiction, right? Mama P suggested I find something productive to do with my time during the day. First, I thought of joining a teen helpline, but I would hate the thought of not being able to help a teen, or worse, causing them more trouble by giving them bad advice. So, I thought of seniors. I have always loved talking to seniors as I find their lives rich and interesting. I came up with the idea to call and speak with seniors. I can't physically visit them, but I can call them on the phone. The more I discussed this budding idea with my MIL, the more excited I became. There is just as much in it for me as there is for them. It would make me feel so good knowing I could put a smile on a lonely senior's face, or brighten their day with a phone call. Some of them never get any visitors. Jason coined it CALLS FOR CARING. So, I will call some nursing homes to pitch my idea.

Update.....my idea has kind of soured....getting a little discouraged as I've called five nursing homes, haven't heard back from two, and three have given me a flat out PASS. I will press on, and try more nursing homes, but I hope someone shares my vision as I am getting very discouraged. I'll keep you updated about this.

I recently joined a book club. It is going to be interesting when I gimp into our first meeting with my poles or walker. I am very self-conscious around people whom I do not know and have to reveal my disease to them for the first time, I always wonder what they think of me. I know this disease is not my fault, but that doesn't make it any less embarrassing. It's at a restaurant for a certain time, so I think I will arrive early to avoid an awkward situation. Hopefully, they will make reservations so that an area is already set up for us.

Update: I ended up texting them that something came up and bailed out on my first book club meeting as my legs felt extra crappy. It's almost like the anticipation of something new amps up my symptoms.

I'm 95% done with Christmas shopping. It's going to be a good Christmas this year. Christmas is a big deal in our family, and the last couple of years have sucked. The year we moved to PEI, we didn't even decorate, and we didn't have 2 nickels to rub together, so Christmas morning we sat on the couch in the living room and I gave the boys all three of their dollar store gifts at once. I didn't even buy for Jason. This year, hopefully will make up for it. The kids have already expressed an interest in having Christmas in the shack, so it should be nice. The shack is a little out building we have on our property that we kind of turned into a fam-cave. We go out there and watch movies, sports,

 or that is where I colour. It's just a nice place to decompress. We got the idea from my Father-In-Law, as he was the originator of the shack idea.... may he rest in peace, and I hope he is looking down on us with love and pride. I wonder if our Christmas tree will fit out there. Probably not...but I'll do some light decorating touches just so you know it's Christmas. I'll even make some breakfast bagels, wrap them in parchment and tinfoil to warm on the fireplace and we can eat after we open gifts.

That is an event to look forward to. See, this is what I was talking about, having an event to look forward to. I love giving gifts and seeing the joy on my kids' faces at the excitement of opening something unexpected. Always looking towards the positive. It has been a bumpy road, but one I think will smoothen out in the next couple of years. At least I can hope. I now have a solid game plan for my health, we are living in this beautiful province, my husband is working at a place that appreciates him as an employee for the first time in his working career and where he can eventually retire from, my children's futures are brighter than ever! My Mother-In-Law is happy as a clam with her new home and her new province, and I'm so glad she moved with us. We also now have the Adventures of Murphy the Moose peppering our days! People always tell me I seem so happy IN SPITE of the fact I have MS. I have bad days that is for sure....but I try not to dwell on them. Sometimes you can't see the rainbow through the shit storm you're living....but it is there I promise you.

I recently texted my brother and told him I missed and loved him. We have not talked much since my Dad died. He was close with him. So was my sister...but it a different way. I am so proud he is living life his way, and raising two beautiful children.

I met with my friend Sukriti the other day, and learned that she is actually an editor. I had no idea when we became friends what she did for a living. Coincidence? I am very thankful I know her. As I said before, I feel like I was meant to write this book. I feel like it is fate that I met her just as I was finishing my book. Since my friend has awoken this writing monster I never knew I had in me....the words are spilling from my brain like vegetables from a cornucopia! I have to move my hand to empty my brain!

Since moving to PEI, I wouldn't say I've necessarily increased my mobility, but my drive is definitely increased. I have gotten a puppy (Murphy-moose) and I am dealing with all the issues surrounding that, I started writing and entering writing contests, started cooking full out meals for the family again, became the resident laundry bitch, and am a knitting prodigy!

MS will not stop me from living.

I believe that what you put out into the world, you get back. I remember a time when I would sit in my backroom in the mornings on Maple Street before going off to the monotonous life of a factory worker, and I would ask over and over that I wanted a closer, less stressed life with my family and a closer relationship with my husband.. I have gotten what I've been asking for. I went from being a factory worker until six years ago, and eventually going off work due to my disability, to moving and living the life in beautiful PEI, discovering my unknown passion for writing, and dare I hope making enough with my first ever published book so my husband never has to work again. I'll be his sugar-mama.

I thank you for joining me on my journey and reading the sometimes mundane occurrences of my every day. As you can tell, I will not let MS dictate my life. I will always fight against it, and I hope that in the future, with healthy eating, clean mindset, and David's exercise program, I will once again have back the abilities that were taken from me because of this horrible disease.

I want you to know that we can hope for a better life, in spite of that scary diagnosis. Things are not always roses and rainbows, sometimes its shit and storms, but you can still find good in most days. Stay positive and keep fighting, friends.

Things work out best, for those who make the best of how things work out.

- John Wooden

We can't always choose the music life plays for us, but we can choose how we dance to it.

- Unknown

Let your hands be so busy catching blessings that there is no room to hold onto grudges.

- unknown

Food for Thought-Are You Going To Eat That?
-a consumer's guide to what your consuming.

Food. My favourite topic.

I love eating food, I love cooking food, I love serving up new recipes to my unsuspecting family.

I have battled up until this point in my life with food. I have only recently began to understand the importance of it, in relation to feeding your body. For nourishment, not pleasure. That it should actually be used to feed your cells and nourish you, and not as a pleasurable habit. That treating it like a pleasurable habit makes it hard to break away from all the delicious snacks, readymade dinners, and fast food. I'm vegan, and it has never been easier to fry up a quick, incredibly delicious vegan burger with all its accompaniments, or to drive to the nearest Burger King or KFC. Most of them have a vegan option now. And they are all equally delicious and addicting. But there is little nutrition in those kinds of foods to feed our hungry cells.

Most people are addicted to food, in all its rich, buttery, sugary, forms. And it's easy to see why. Would you rather have a cheesy pizza or a salad? A delicious burger with fries, or a salad? My vote would have laid with the cheesy pizza, burger and fries just a little while ago. In watching the many documentaries on plant-based eating, I have realized that we have to give the body what it needs, or we will develop disease after years upon years of neglect. Case in point....I have MS. I truly believe that my devil may care attitude towards what I fed my body, with a dash of childhood trauma and a sprinkling of viruses in my early childhood are what set my disease in motion. Combine that with my years of treating my body like a brewery and not caring about sleep, and you have a recipe for disaster. How can I possibly know that my body is craving nutrients and hydration, and not give it what it needs? Cookies are delicious, but so is a really ripe piece of watermelon......

And so this book was born.

Our diets have changed drastically over the past 100 years. Processed food was never really an option before. Now everything is at our fingertips. But most of the convenience foods are not foods at all, but great imitators, designed to keep us reaching into that bag. They are specifically engineered to keep us craving that sugar, salt, fat ratio that has been so cleverly designed to spur those cravings. I went plant-based specifically to treat my disease. But eventually changed to being vegan, not really caring what I was shoving in my trap, as long as it wasn't anything previously living. I was not giving my body what it needed to work at optimal performance. That is the major difference between being vegan and being plant based. Vegans do not eat meat as they do not want to kill animals. They try and avoid anything that causes the death and misery of an innocent living animal, but they will eat processed plant crap and not think twice about it. As long as they're not killing an animal.

Whole food plant-based, in my humble opinion, is something we do for our health, because we know that eating meat and dairy will eventually catch up with us. Not only that, it is not as bad for the environment. If you're plant-based. There

 is no cow in the field excreting a quarter of its weight in shit daily. (Google credit: a 750lb cow produces roughly 65lbs of shit daily. If you have 30 cows in your pasture, that's 1950 lbs. of shit a day!) That's a lot of methane creeping into our environment, and that is just one farmers field in this world.....that doesn't include the masses of animals in factory farming. All over the globe. Scary. It is easy to see why that surpasses the detriment that cars cause in CO2 emissions. I would say I'm a mix of both. I'm a plant-based vegan. I know that plants are the way to go, and what our bodies use most efficiently, but I also couldn't imagine taking someone's life, just because I wanted that momentary taste in my mouth.

Our diets have taken a turn for the worse over the last 75-80 years since WWII. After the war, the shelved food revolution began, in which a lot of our meals derived from convenience and not necessity. There were emulsifiers, additives, stabilizers, preservatives, thickeners, anti-caking agents, and antimicrobial elements, all added to our foods to make them more shelf stable. Not to mention an increase in the sugar, salt, fat ratio in order to make the food craveable and addicting. We have never been unhealthier, while at the same time having everything within our reach. We no longer have to hunt our next meal, we don't have to scrounge for berries and edible plants because we now have 24 hr. grocery stores and food is incredibly easy to obtain in this day and age. It is refrigerated and packaged in such a way that it is at the ready. We just have to grab it out of the fridge or off of the shelf. We KNOW what is healthy....fruits and vegetables....yet most of us avoid them like the plague because they do not satisfy that craving for the sugar, salt, and fat that we have become accustomed to eating.

If we do not break from that pattern of satisfying our every edible desire, then we may be leading ourselves down a path of inevitable disease and health decline, not to mention, more importantly, the end of this planet. You hear about the odd anomalies of people that smoked until they were 82, and had sausage every morning for breakfast, but for the vast majority of people, if we do not take our diets seriously, and we choose to eat strictly for taste, it will catch up with us.....eventually.

A lot of people, when they have been vegan for a while, wonder how they ever ate a product associated with a beautiful living being. My hope is that more and more people switch from being meat eaters to being vegan, and eventually transitioning to plant-based, where you eat to live, not live to eat. Because let's face it, being vegan isn't really healing or healthy if one is a junk-food vegan. You still have to take into consideration there are fat, chemicals, unhealthy oils in some processed vegan foods, and they should be treated like an occasional treat.

My sister and I have always struggled with our weight. I developed MS, and that led me to go whole food plant-based, full out Forks Over Knives way of eating....I think watching the documentary really sealed the deal for me. But, after being plant-based and eating really clean for a couple years following my diagnosis, I began transitioning to a more to processed food and calorie heavy vegan diet. Now looking back, had I stayed more whole food plant-based ....I think I would have less physical detriments than I do now. As I said before, crap food is crap food, doesn't matter that it's made from plants or not.

This is the same way, and I've never spoken this aloud, so it's a little ironic that I'm choosing to put it in my book, for dare I hope millions to read, but I believe that my sister gave herself Fibromyalgia. She got it AFTER she got stomach surgery to save her eye. Her doctors told her that she may lose the sight in her eye or eyes because the pressure in her brain was too high due to her weight.. I think I'm describing it correctly. So, she went to the States to have a radical stomach bypass that forced her to drop weight rapidly to relieve the pressure and avoid the potential blindness. I don't blame her because I'm sure that must have been a scary thing to hear, so you would want to do whatever you could to definitely avoid that. But I also honestly believe, from everything I've learned about nutrition, that the drop in nutrient intake that occurs after that particular surgery and the fact that you're altering the way your body processes food can be extremely detrimental to your health. Especially if you don't follow a strict eating regimen. There is a strict protocol to adhere to following that surgery. I often wonder if my sister would have just gone on a really healthful diet and drank her water, if she would have avoided not only the exploding eyeballs, but her monkey that she now has to take care of for life....Fibromyalgia. Now, I'm no doctor, and I am not doling out medical advice here, but that is just my humble opinion from all the things I've learned about food since really needing to pay attention to it.

(Disclaimer: This is just my personal feelings, not based on any scientific findings.)

One of my favourite things to do is to go online to any number of the vegan sites I belong to...is to argue the point of a plant-based diet with the meat-eating people who scroll and troll on my vegan sites. I know it's immature and juvenile of me, but it's like getting the last word in an argument when you know you are 100% right. People don't want to hear about veganism or plant-based diets and how it's better for our health and the planet because we are not raising all that cattle who shit and fart into our atmosphere, exacerbating the already extensive climate crisis. They want to continue their traditions as a lot of the time it is inherited ignorance that they continue the cycle off of. But it is their choice. It is the same with my own family. We all used to be staunch plant-based vegans. Since moving to an island where the major industry is fishing, the kids and Jason have chosen, on occasion, to eat fish and seafood and be more pescatarian because, let's face it, it is delicious. Absolutely delicious. I myself will never change from plant-based vegan because I can never imagine taking anyone's life for a fleeting moment of pleasure for my taste buds. But hey, that's just me. They eat mostly vegan, which is better than not. But again, getting side-tracked... I love arguing these points online. You have to choose your own way of eating, but just do your research and arm yourself with knowledge. It has never been easier to eat healthfully. Try and eat for health, not for pleasure. Capture pleasure in different ways...by going for a walk with a loved one, taking a relaxing bath, or playing fetch with your dog.

"Eat to live, and don't live to eat." ~ Benjamin Franklin.

-
-

Distraction is the enemy of intention.

- Nicole Tracey

A smooth sea never made a skilled sailor.

- Franklin D. Roosevelt

You get what you focus on, so focus on what you want.

- Tiny Positive

Naughty and Nice Recipes

I developed a love of cooking from my father, so this section is dedicated to him.

A lot of the recipes that follow, I've tweaked from recipes I've found online, or they are tried and true recipes passed down through the generations that I have veganized, or I simply created them myself. The photos that accompany each recipe are mine. I wanted all the pictures in my book to be my own, not professionally shot. All of my pics were taken with a 6 year old Samsung phone with no downloaded filter apps. I wanted this book to be as real and authentic as possible. I think they look pretty yummy, and I hope you do too.

I hope you enjoy these recipes and tweak them to create your own masterpieces! I have separated them with a little angel and little devil symbol as it helps me decide how naughty or nice I want to be that day.

The little angel recipes are more whole food plant forward and less processed, whereas the little devil recipes use more processed foods like Beyond Meat. They are still vegan recipes, and they are without meat and dairy, which I guess makes them a bit healthier, albeit still processed.

The devil recipes are definitely not for everyday consumption......I can still gain weight if I eat them too frequently. Sometimes you may see an angel and a devil together...and that simply means I can adjust the ingredients to my liking, to minimize the processed ingredients and make it a little healthier if that's what I choose to do.. But you can use them to your liking, and adapt and create your own dishes!

Note: The miscellaneous section contains recipes that are utilized throughout the cookbook.

*Nooch=Nutritional yeast. Nutritional yeast is a staple of vegan cooking. It is a delicious cheesy-tasting powder used in LOTS of vegan recipes..so if you see me talking about nooch, that's what it is....

If you can change your mind, you can change your life.

- William James

Intense love does not measure. It just gives.

- Mother Teresa

Strength is what we gain from the madness we survive.

- HNasty

Appetizers

Appetizers

1. Overnight veggie salsa
3. Spinach and Artichoke Dip
4. Stuffed Mushroom Caps
5. Addictive Chip Dip
6. Taco Roll ups
7. Pizza Rolls
8. Garlic Bread Focaccia
9. Karen C's Hummus
10. 7 Layer Dip

Overnight veggie salsa

One of my husband's favourites. A great go to appetizer! Flavourful and healthy with fresh vegetables and hearty beans.

- 1 pkg Knorr vegetable soup mix
- 1/3 c boiling water
- 3 lrg tomatoes, seeded and diced
- ¾ c each corn and black beans
- ½ red onion, diced
- ½ diced and seeded jalapeno
- 2 Tbsp. cilantro, chopped
- 1 Tbsp. lime juice
- 1 Tbsp. flax oil
- 1 clove garlic, minced
- 2 tsp. jalapeno's seeds removed and diced

Combine soup mix with boiling water. Cover 10 min.

Stir in remaining ingredients, cover, and sit overnight in fridge.

Serve with tortilla chips

Spinach and Artichoke Dip

This recipe is off the hook delicious! It pleases any palate, great for vegans and meat eaters alike!

- 1 1/2 c Cashews
- 4 cloves garlic, minced
- 1 small onion, minced
- 4 c spinach, chopped
- 2 Tbsp. vegetable broth
- 2 cans Artichoke hearts chopped
- 1 1/2 c Plant milk of choice
- 1 lemon juiced
- 1 c vegan shredded mozzarella and 1 c vegan shredded cheddar- I like Violife!
- 1/4 c Nutritional Yeast
- 1 lemon, juiced
- 1 1/2 tsp. salt

Preheat oven to 425°. Sauté garlic and onion in a little vegetable broth until cooked.

(If you do not have a Vitamix, soak cashews in boiling water for 1hr before using. Drain.)

To high powered blender, add Cashews, milk, nutritional yeast, lemon juice, and salt. Blend until smooth.

In food processor pulse spinach and Artichokes until broken down a bit. You still want it kind of chunky.

Put cashew mixture in bowl with artichokes and spinach, add garlic and onion mixture, 3/4 of shredded cheeses, mix.

Pour in 8x8 casserole. Top with remaining shredded cheeses, bake for 25 minutes.

Serve with Tortilla chips

Stuffed mushroom caps

I have this as both naughty and nice. For nice recipe omit beyond meat and cheese and use the chopped up mushroom stems, other veg you'd like and nutritional yeast. Classic party app, it will leave guests coming back for more...

Preheat oven to 375°.

- Clean stuffer mushrooms, remove, and chop stems and put aside for later.
- 1 onion, diced
- 1 clove garlic, minced
- 1 zucchini, diced
- 1 Plant based burger, (I like Beyond) cooked and crumbled-I used 2 or 3 burgers
- 1/2 c vegan shredded mozzarella
- 2 Tbsp. vegetable broth
- 2 Tbsp. Nutritional Yeast
- Mushroom stems cleaned, and chopped

Sauté mushroom stems, onions, garlic, zucchini, crumbled vegan burger in broth until broken down and burger and onion is cooked.

Mix in vegan mozzarella while mixture is still warm. Stuff mushroom caps with mixture and place on baking tray.

Top each with a little nutritional yeast and bake for 20 minutes.

Addictive Chip Dip

Who doesn't like a good chip dip? And with no dairy, it makes it a healthier choice. You'd never know it contains no dairy, as it's so creamy and delicious. Eat it with vegetables for a healthy snack!!

- 1 c cashews
- 1 tsp. garlic powder
- Juice of 1 lemon
- 3/4 to 2 c water
- 1 Tbsp. Nutritional Yeast
- 1 pkg onion soup mix or your own recipe
- 1 Tbsp. parsley
- You can also mix it up by adding 1 Tbsp. of dill weed

Soak Cashews in boiling water for 1 hr. if you don't have a Vitamix. Drain

Put in high powered blender with rest of ingredients. Blend until smooth.

Remove and serve with chips, or chopped vegetables.

Taco Roll ups

These are a great party app when you want to spend more time with your guests....make them ahead!

- 8oz vegan cream cheese mixed with 1 c vegan sour cream-see recipe in Misc.
- 2 green onions, chopped small
- ½ c chopped green olives
- 2 Tbsp. Taco seasoning
- ½ c diced tomatoes, skin only
- 2 c vegan shredded cheddar
- Tortillas

Mix all.

Spread on Tortillas, roll up tightly in saran wrap, and refrigerate 2 hrs.

Slice and serve.

Pizza Rolls

You don't have to take off your pajamas to answer the door with this recipe. Takes a little time, but so worth it!

- 300ml warm water
- 1 pkg yeast or 2 1/4 tsp.
- 1 tsp. sugar
- 2 tsp. salt
- 3 c + 2 Tbsp. flour

Combine first 4 ingredients. Proof yeast. Once proofed, mix with 3 c flour, form dough. Set aside to rise for 1 hour.

- Vegan mozzarella- I like Violife
- Tomato sauce spiced with basil, oregano, fresh minced garlic to taste
- Cooked, crumbled plant based meat -I like Beyond
- Black olives in desired amount

Preheat oven 350°

Sprinkle 2 Tbsp. of flour on work surface Roll proofed dough to rectangle about 1/4" thick. Top with sauce. Sprinkle with mozzarella, crumbled Beyond and other toppings. Roll up into log.

Cut into slices, lay face up on sheet. Cover with towel. Let rise again until doubled. Bake for 25-30 min

Garlic Bread Focaccia

An impressive appetizer that beats take out any day of the week. Dip in marinara or pizza sauce for extra flavour!

1 pkg yeast (2 1/4 tsp.)
1 c warm water
½ tsp. sugar
½ tsp. salt
5-7 c flour- divided
2 Tbsp. Extra virgin olive oil
Vegan butter in desired amount
Garlic salt in desired amount
Pizza sauce for dipping

Proof yeast with sugar and warm water in stand mixer bowl. Let sit 10 minutes until yeast is in full bloom.
Add In olive oil and salt. Stir. Put on stand mixer and add in 2 ½ c of flour. Mix until combined. Add in the rest of the flour 1 cup at a time until the dough comes away from the bowl clean. Put in oiled bowl, making sure the oil coats the whole ball of dough. Cover bowl with a towel and let rise 1 hour. Take dough out on floured surface. Cut in half. Roll out dough to desired

thickness, put on pizza stone. Do the same with the
other ½ of dough. Let rise 20 minutes.
Melt butter, mix in a bit of garlic salt, brush on focaccia.
Bake at 450* for 15-20 minutes. Remove, let cool 5 minutes, and slice. Dip in pizza sauce if desired

Karen C's Hummus

I used to work with a lady that made the most amazing hummus.

An incredibly easy recipe to whip up, and it is so flavourful! Swap the olive oil for flax oil and enjoy with fresh vegetables for an extra healthy option!

In a blender or food processor mix;

2 cans of rinsed chickpeas

3 cloves of garlic

Juice of one lemon, or to taste- I like 2 lemons

4oz of warm water

½ Tbsp. tahini paste, plus 1 Tbsp. of the liquid

Salt to taste

1 T of Olive oil, (you could do flax oil here for extra health. My suggestion, not Karen's)

Blend. Put in shallow bottomed dish. Drizzle top with 1 tsp. of olive or flax oil

Serve with warm naan, or fresh cut vegetables.

7 Layer Dip

A great party appetizer that is fun and easy to throw together!

2 cans of black beans, rinsed, drained and mashed

Mix beans with 1 Tbsp. each of smoked paprika, garlic powder

2 c of guacamole

2 c of easy cashew queso-Recipe in Apps

2 c Shredded Romaine, Spinach or Kale

1 c Vegan Sour Cream-Recipe in Misc.

3-5 Green onions, chopped

1 c Green or black olives, sliced

Tortilla Chips for dipping

In casserole dish, layer in order. Enjoy with tortilla chips.

Courage is not having the strength to go on; it's going on when you don't have the strength

-Theodore Roosevelt

Every day is a new beginning, take a deep breath, smile and start again.
-Tamara Kulish

Life is short, break the rules. Forgive quickly, love truly, kiss slowly, laugh uncontrollably, and never regret anything that made you smile
- Mark Twain

Soups

Soups

1. Nick's Veggie Soup
2. King Oyster Scallop Chowder
3. Lasagna Stoup
4. Vegan Beef Barley
5. Vegan Italian Wedding Soup
6. Magnificent Mushroom Soup
7. 30 Minute Coconut Curry
8. Avegolmono
9. Nick's Smoky bean soup
10. Classic French Onion

Nick's Veggie Soup

This reminds me of the canned condensed soup that I used to have for lunch on school days. Delicious memory meal copycatted.

12 c of vegetable broth
3 cans of tomato sauce (398ml)
1 large potato diced, or 3 medium
1½ c frozen peas, carrots, corn.
1 diced onion
A handful of chopped spinach
1½ c of alphabet noodles
Diced smoked tofu
Maple syrup to taste
Nutritional yeast to taste
2 tsp. thyme
1 Tbsp. parsley
Salt and pepper to taste

Add broth and tomato sauce to large pot. Flavour with salt and pepper. Add thyme, parsley, maple syrup, and nutritional yeast. Adjust seasonings. Add diced vegetables. Bring to a boil, simmer 30 minutes. Make sure veg is soft, add tofu cubes, noodles and spinach. Cook 10 minutes.

Serve with hillbilly hot rolls.

King Oyster Scallop Chowder

The King Oyster Scallops are the stars of this soup, so much so, you will forget that they are mushrooms! Delicious company- impressing soup that you can serve to anyone with a seafood allergy!

12 c vegetable broth
1 sweet onion, chopped
3 ribs of diced celery
5 large garlic cloves, minced
3 ½ c large diced potato
½ c diced shiitake
1 tsp. fresh rosemary
2 c plant based milk
1 c diced carrot
1 c peas
¾ c corn
1 Tbsp. tamari
3 Tbsp. dulse
Salt and pepper
Pinch of red pepper flakes
Parsley to taste

King Oyster Mushroom Scallops (recipe in Misc.)
Sauté onion, celery, potato, carrot and rosemary.
Add stock and corn and peas.
Over medium high heat, bring to a boil, cook 15 minutes. Partially blend with hand blender. Add parsley.

Lasagna Stoup

I call it a stoup because it's a cross between a stew and a soup! A delicious, "stick to your ribs" meal that is hearty and flavourful. Enjoy with rustic fresh homemade bread to sop up every bit of deliciousness!

4 plant based burgers (I used Beyond)
1 sweet onion, chopped
2 cloves garlic, minced
3 ribs celery, diced
2 15oz cans of tomato puree
12 c vegetable broth
Italian Seasoning to taste
1 pkg cooked lasagna noodles-roughly chopped
1 can of black olives, drained
Shredded Vegan Mozzarella to top- (I like Violife)

Sauté onion, garlic, celery until soft. Crumble and cook burgers. Break up. Cook through stirring occasionally. Add tomato puree, broth, seasonings.
Bring to boil, turn to low.

Vegan "Beef" Barley

Another of my husband's favourites. Curl up with a bowl of this on a blustery day and feel warm and toasty inside!

1 onion, diced
2 Ribs celery, diced
2 carrots, diced
2 garlic cloves, minced
1 c seitan, diced or Beyond meat cooked, crumbled
½ c red wine
6 c vegetable broth
1 14oz can of diced tomatoes
½ c pearl barley
2 bay leaves
Thyme to taste
Salt and pepper to taste
Parsley for finishing

Sauté vegetables, adding a little broth to the pan. Add seitan, sauté a few more minutes. Add red wine, simmer. Reduce by ½. Add broth, tomatoes, barley and herbs. Bring to a boil. Reduce to simmer, and simmer for 40-50 minutes until barley is tender. Serve with fresh baked bread.

Vegan Italian wedding Soup

This recipe is a little time consuming because you have to make the tiny meatballs, but it is so worth it in the end. Impresses...everytime.

8 c water
1 small onion, diced
3 cloves garlic, minced
2 carrots, diced
2 ribs celery, diced
1 ½ Tbsp. of Italian seasoning
2 bay leaves
Salt and pepper to taste
3 c spinach, chopped
1 c orzo
4 Tbsp. Nutritional yeast
2 Tbsp. garlic powder
1 Tbsp. onion powder
1 Tbsp. oregano
Plant based ground meat (I used Beyond- 4 Burgers)
Vegan Parmesan
Fresh parsley

Mix plant based meat in bowl with parmesan, garlic powder, onion powder, oregano and salt and pepper. Make meatballs. (I like them really tiny, but it is more time consuming, so make them to your taste, I sometimes am so lazy, that I'll just brown the Beyond, and add it as is. Still tastes delicious.)

Bake meatballs on cookie sheet @ 375* for 10 minutes if your making tiny ones. Increase time if making larger meatballs. You want them browned. In a large pot, sauté vegetables in a little bit of broth until fork tender. Add spices, liquids and pasta. Bring to a boil. Turn down to a simmer, add meatballs and parsley, heat through and then serve warm.

Magnificent Mushroom Soup

A mushroom lover's soup, thick and creamy, it is incredibly flavourful and satisfying!

4 Portobello mushrooms, diced
A big handful of shiitake
1 small pkg of cremini mushrooms
1 small pkg of white
Any other mixes you desire (can never have too many mushrooms, right?)
¼ c whole wheat flour
8 c vegetable broth
1 Tbsp. tamari
2 shallots, minced
2 garlic cloves, minced
1 tsp. thyme
1 ½ c plant milk
2 Tbsp. Nutritional yeast
Salt and pepper to taste

Dice all mushrooms. If using any dry mixes, reconstitute in water, and save soaking water. In large pot, add a bit of broth, thyme, shallots, garlic, and sauté. Add mushrooms, even soaking water if used, tamari, flour and cook them down until they are cooked through and soft. Remove some for adding back to soup. Add milk to mushrooms in pot and puree with hand blender. Add nutritional yeast and saved mushrooms. Season to taste.

Thirty Minute Coconut Curry

This soup has so many different levels that surprise you at every turn. Complex and flavourful, it will make you go back for another bowl!

1 small onion, chopped
4 cloves garlic, minced
1 Tbsp. grated fresh ginger
Handful of bean sprouts
½ c diced carrots
¼ c diced tomatoes
1/3 c snow peas
1 Tbsp. curry powder
2 14oz coconut milk
6 c veggie stock
Salt and pepper
Handful of fresh spinach
Pinch of cayenne
Thai curry paste

Saute onion, garlic, ginger, carrot, and snow peas for a few minutes. Season. Add curry, cayenne, and liquids. Simmer for 15 minutes. Add tomatoes, rice noodles and spinach.

Taste and adjust seasonings. Simmer until noodles are soft.

Avegolmono

One of my favourite soups, lemony and light, it is a delicious soup any day of the week.

3 leeks, cleaned well and chopped

1 onion, diced

5 carrots, diced

4 cloves garlic, minced

8 c vegetable broth

¾ c orzo

2 lemons, juiced

Parsley, chopped

Sauté leeks, onion, and garlic. Cook 5 minutes. Add carrots, stir, and cook 5 more minutes. Add broth and bring to a boil, add orzo, reduce to medium. Cook 9 minutes. Add in lemon juice and parsley.

Nick's Smoky bean soup

A hearty, flavourful soup that will warm your cockles and stick to your ribs! This is another recipe to serve with a crusty bread to sop up all the beany deliciousness!

2 cans of chickpeas, 1 undrained
2 cans of black beans, 1 undrained
1 can of kidney beans, pulse in food processor
1 large onion, diced
2 carrots, diced
3 ribs of celery, diced
12 c vegetable broth
6 cloves garlic, minced
2 pkgs Yves ham, diced
Nutritional yeast to taste
Garlic and onion powder to taste
Fresh sage
3 potatoes, diced
1 can coconut milk

Saute carrots, celery, onion, potatoes and garlic in a little vegetable broth.
Add rest of ingredients and bring to a boil, turn down heat to a simmer.
Simmer until vegetables are soft.

Serve with crusty bread.

Classic French Onion

Caramelized onions, with a rich vegetable broth, topped with crisped baguette and vegan mozzarella. It doesn't get any better than this!

3 Tbsp. vegan butter

1 Tbsp. olive oil

5 large sweet onions, sliced

1 tsp. salt

½ tsp. pepper

1 c white wine

2 Tbsp. flour

6 cups vegetable broth

2 Tbsp. of better than bouillon veg paste

1 tsp. vegan worcestershire

¾ t fresh thyme

2 bay leaves

Tamari

Garlic powder

1 baguette, sliced in ½" slices

2 c vegan mozzarella

½ c nutritional yeast

In a large dutch oven, melt butter over medium heat. Add the oil and onions. Season with salt and pepper, cook until the onions are caramelized, about 40-45 min. You may need to add a bit of oil from occasionally to prevent burning. Deglaze pan with white wine, scraping up bits that stick. When wine has evaporated, add the vegetable broth and veg paste. Stir to dissolve. Simmer 30 minutes. While broth is simmering, cut and butter baguette with vegan butter. Sprinkle with a bit of garlic powder. Put them on baking sheet. Bake for 10 minutes at 400*.

Taste and adjust soup. Add Bragg's for deeper flavour. Ladle into French onion soup bowls, top with baguette slice and a handful of vegan mozzarella and sprinkle of nutritional yeast. Broil at 400* until cheese is melted and bubbly about 5-7 minutes.

Carefully remove from oven. Enjoy.

Procrastination is the grave in which opportunity is buried.

- Alyce Cornyn-Selby

Today is your opportunity to build the tomorrow you want

- Ken Poirot

Every day may not be good, but there is something good in everyday.

- Alice Morse Earl

Side Dishes

Side Dishes

1. Instant Pot Mashed Potatoes
2. Mediterranean Orzo Salad
4. Roasted Tray of Veg
5. Cold Quinoa Salad
6. White Wine and Garlic Mushrooms
8. Spanish Bean Salad
9. Roasted Cauliflower
10. Sauerkraut and Sausage

Instant Pot Mashed Potatoes

Who doesn't love mashed potatoes? This is a quick and easy side dish that can go along side and any main. Comes together very quickly, so it's one of those recipes you'll always want to keep in your recipe book.

6-7 medium potatoes

Water to cover potatoes

2 tsp. salt

¼ c. vegan butter

¼ vegan sour cream

¼ c plant milk

Garlic powder to taste

Onion powder to taste

Pepper to taste

Chopped fresh thyme and parsley

Chop potatoes, put in Instant Pot. Cover with water, Cook on manual- 8 min

Quick release, drain water, add all ingredients to desired taste, mash.

Mediterranean Orzo Salad

Do not lose this recipe. It is one of my family's favourite things to stuff their face with when their hungry. It's so convenient because you can eat it cold right from the fridge! Throw in your favourite toppings!

2 pkgs orzo pasta
1 ½ c diced tomatoes
½ c black olives
1 red pepper, diced
1 red onion, diced
½ c vegan feta (I use Violife)
½ c fresh parsley
2 Tbsp. capers

Dressing:
1 c flax oil (you can use olive, but it will have a different flavour)
Juice from 2 lemons
Salt and pepper
1 clove garlic, minced
½ tsp. maple syrup
Nutritional yeast to taste
Put in jar and shake

Cook orzo until al dente. Drain, put orzo in big bowl, and mix in all other ingredients. Add dressing, toss to coat. Season with salt and pepper. Taste and adjust seasonings to your desired taste. Serve cold.

Roasted Tray of Veg

A good mix of veg that gets nice and browned in the oven. Put them on a cute serving tray for an impressive display!

1 lb. red potatoes (about 4 c)
1 lrg onion, cut in quarters
2 medium carrots, cut in bite size pcs
1 medium bell pepper, quartered
1 medium zucchini, chunked
1 pkg mushrooms, halved
1/4 c olive oil
2 tsp. chopped garlic
1 tsp. dried thyme
1 tsp. dried tarragon
½ tsp. salt
¼ tsp. pepper

400* Mix all in bowl. Put potatoes and carrots in one dish. Toss with half the olive oil and spices. Mix to coat. Put on cookie sheet, bake 10 min. Toss bell pepper, zucchini, mushrooms and onions with other half of olive oil and spices. Put on tray with potatoes and carrots. Bake 30-35 minutes until tender. Stir halfway through cooking.

Cold Quinoa Salad

A nice healthy salad. Perfect for a picnic or lunch during a hike. A nutritious, energy packed salad that will keep you motivated to keep moving!

1 c quinoa
2 c water
1 English cucumber, diced
1 red pepper diced
1 red onion diced
Smoked tofu, cubed
1 ½ tsp. red wine vinegar
1 ½ tsp. balsamic vinegar
1 tsp. each of garlic and onion powder
1 tsp. salt and pepper
1 tsp. dried parsley

Cook quinoa to pkg directions. Add rest of ingredients and toss. Refrigerate 1 hour.

White wine and Garlic Mushrooms

A delicious sautéed mushroom is one of my favourite things. Throw some wine and garlic in the mix, and your talking my kind of side. Always delicious, meaty and flavourful, this side is sure to impress!

2 c mushrooms of choice

1 head of garlic

2 Tbsp. vegan butter

1 c white wine

Fresh herbs of choice, I like parsley, thyme, rosemary.

Salt and pepper to taste

Mince garlic. Melt butter in pan. Sauté mushrooms, add herbs and garlic. Add wine. Simmer until it reduces by half. Season with salt and pepper.

Spanish Bean Salad

Looking for something substantial? This is a hearty dish that is not only good for you, but fills you up!

1 can mixed beans

1 can of chickpeas

1 can of white kidney beans

1 red bell pepper, diced

2 carrots, diced

2 celery, diced

2 green onions, chopped

2 Tbsp. fresh lime juice

2 Tbsp. white wine vinegar

2 Tbsp. fresh lemon juice

2 Tbsp. maple syrup

Salt and pepper to taste

1 tsp. chili powder

2 cloves garlic, minced

Fresh cilantro or parsley

Mix all. For an even healthier option serve over a bed of greens!

Roasted Cauliflower

I can always get my kids to eat their veggies when I cook up some roasted cauliflower! It's a sure hit!

1 medium cauliflower, chopped in florets

4 Tbsp. Olive oil

Salt and pepper to taste

Smoked paprika to taste

Garlic powder to taste

Put cauliflower in a bowl. Drizzle with olive oil. Sprinkle on above spices. Mix. Repeat.

Place seasoned cauliflower on tray, bake for 15-25 minutes until desired doneness.

Sauerkraut and Sausage

O.K.....for real. This is one of those recipes that everyone who tries it will want. It is amazing on vegan hotdogs and sausages, or sitting atop scrambled vegan eggs and just about anything you place it next to on your plate. It's sooo good.

2 jars of wine sauerkraut, rinsed and drained

2 15oz cans of diced tomatoes

1 sweet onion, chopped

1 pkg of Beyond Sausage, grilled and sliced (you can use cooked tempeh and tofu for a healthier option)

Chopped and cooked vegan bacon

Mix all. Place in 300* oven for 3-4 hours, stirring every so often. Remove when recipe has lost its juices, and it has a nice golden colour.

One day you will wake up and there will be no more time to do the things you have always dreamed of. Do them now.

- Paula Coelho

Do the best you can until you know better, then when you know better, do better.

- Maya Angelou

The doctor of the future will no longer treat the human frame with drugs, but rather will cure and prevent disease with nutrition.

- Thomas Edison

Sandwiches

Sandwiches

1. Nick's Dagwood
2. Sauerkraut Hoagie
3. Old School Hot "Turkey" Sandwich
4. BBQ'D Tofu Sammie with creamy coleslaw
5. Classic Meatball Sub
6. Magnificent Muffaletta
7. Breakfast Bagel

Nick's Dagwood

A good sandwich is underrated. Whenever I go out to a restaurant, I invariably look for a nice sandwich. The name of this one is description enough.

Thick sliced homemade bread (killer recipe in baked goods)
Vegan butter
Vegan Mayo on one half. (You can make your own cashew mayo, or you can use with Hellman's vegan mayo)
Violife mature cheddar, or another vegan cheese (You could use a light layer of Smoky Cheddar cheese found in Misc. as an angel option)
Vegan turkey lunchmeat
Sliced smoked tofu
Yves salami
Violife mature cheddar
Sliced red onion
Sliced dill pickle
Chopped olives
Very thinly sliced tomato
A crisp lettuce, like a nice romaine

Slice bread thickly. Layer in order with the listed menu items. Enjoy the deliciousness that is my version of a Dagwood!

Sauerkraut Hoagie

Perfect for a lazy day, you can wrap these in parchment and tinfoil, and pop them in a cooler for a nice picnic sandwich. Just make sure you use a sturdy bun to stand up against the sauerkraut.

Nice sturdy hoagie bun
Sliced smoked tofu
Sauerkraut and sausage (in Side dishes)
Mustard

Cover bread with tofu slices. Top with a couple of Tbsp's of sauerkraut and sausage, and some mustard. Enjoy with a nice salad or side of French fries!

Old school hot "turkey" sandwich

I debated including this recipe, as my husband said it is a dated meal option.....but I disagree....I think it is a deliciously satisfying recipe that stands the test of time!!!

Homemade bread (recipe in baked goods) sliced thickly

Sliced smoked tofu

Sautéed mushrooms and onions

Vegan gravy of choice

Saute mushrooms and onions until soft and done to your liking.   Smoke tofu. Let cool. Slice tofu, put on buttered bread. Make gravy of choice. Top tofu with mushrooms and onions, and some delicious gravy! Dive in!

BBQ'D Tofu Sammie with Creamy Coleslaw

This recipe was born because I just wanted something different one day. The bbq sauce becomes caramelized to the tofu, creating an extra layer of deliciousness! This sandwich is over the top.

Sturdy ciabatta
Smoked sliced tofu
Creamy Vegan Coleslaw
Your favourite bbq sauce

Smoke tofu. (recipe in misc.) Let cool. Slice lengthwise as thick as desired. Place on pre-heated grill pan. Cook on medium. Brush with bbq sauce. Cook a couple minutes, flip. Brush with more bbq sauce. Cook 2 minutes. Continue to flip, baste and cook until desired texture is achieved. Remove and place on ciabatta with a serving of creamy coleslaw.

Classic Meatball Sub

I prefer this with a product like Beyond, but you could certainly health it up if you have a tried and tested "healthy meatball."

Regardless of what you use, It's hard not to make it delicious when it's coated in sauce and stuffed in a sub!

Sturdy sub of choice

Pkg of Beyond or plant based meat of choice

Binders and herbs: Breadcrumbs, herbs of choice, garlic powder, smoked paprika

Spaghetti sauce of choice

Vegan Mozzarella (use smoky cheddar if you want a healthier option)

If using a product like Beyond, put meat in bowl, and throw in what you like for spices. There is no need for measurements. Mix. Form meatballs by using 1 Tbsp of meat and make meatball. Brown meatballs in oven. 400* for 25 minutes. Put meatballs in large skillet add your favourite sauce and simmer them for around 25 minutes. Toast a sub bun in oven (400*) until lightly browned. Top bun with simmered meatballs and sprinkle with vegan mozzarella. Put in broiler until cheese is melty and delicious!

Magnificent Muffaletta

This is hands down my husband's favourite sandwich. Originating in New Orleans in 1906, this sandwich is definitely a game changer. It will satisfy your carbo-licious cravings!!

Ring loaf or sturdy ciabatta
2 T of red wine vinegar
Vegan provolone
Vegan turkey
Vegan salami
Romaine lettuce
Sliced red onion
½ c Chopped olives

Chop olives into tiny pieces. Add the red wine vinegar and let sit 5 minutes. Hollow out ring loaf or ciabatta so you have a place for the chopped olives to live. Layer in order of ingredients. Put top loaf on, wrap and press in fridge with weight of choice (I use a plate with a couple heavy cans) for a couple hours to let the flavours amalgamate. Enjoy with chips and cut veggies.

Breakfast Bagel

Sometimes I awake in the morning and have a hunger like a bear who has just awoke from hibernation. This sandwich hits the spot and will satisfy that craving! (You can omit the processed vegan meat and use smoked tofu with smoky cheddar cheese to replace the processed ingredients for a healthier choice)

Multigrain bagel
Vegan butter
Mature vegan cheddar slice
Just egg or something similar
Beyond sausage patty
Vegan Hollandaise (recipe in Misc.)

Cook sausage according to pkg directions. Make hollandaise. Toast bagel. Heat egg. Butter toasted bagel, put on cheese, sausage and egg. Top egg with a Tbsp. of that delicious hollandaise! Enjoy the trip to flavour town.

You don't always need a plan. Sometimes you just need to breathe, trust, let go, and see what happens.
 - Mandy Hale

The moment you're ready to quit, is usually the moment right before the miracle happens.

Don't give up.

- Unknown

Don't let anyone who hasn't been in your shoes, tell you how to tie your laces.

- Unknown

Entrees

Entrees

1. Dirty Rice
2. Zucchini Ravioli
3. Chick'n Pot Pie
4. Cincinnati Style Chili
5. BBQ Tofu
6. Beef Stroganoff
7. Black Bean Quesadillas
8. Tortiere
9. King Oyster Mushroom Scallops
10. Smoked Tofu Ciabattas
11. Loaded Coleslaw Pitas
12. Buddha Bowls
13. Overnight Alfredo
14. Taco Salad
15. Hungaloo
16. Foccacia Pizza

Dirty Rice

This is one of my favourite Instant Pot recipes. It comes together so easy, is always a hit with my family and can be made with a product like Beyond Meat, or cubed smoked tofu, depending on your mood. Don't be afraid to spice it up if you can handle it.

4 c basmati rice
4 c vegetable broth
1 onion, diced
1 c of Edamame
1 red pepper, diced
Vegetable broth for sautéing
1 c corn
2 grated carrots
2 ribs celery, diced
Sliced mushrooms
1 pkg of beyond burger, sausage, plant based chicken, or smoked tofu
2 Tbsp. garlic powder
1 Tbsp. chili powder
Salt and pepper to taste
1 tsp. Basil and oregano

In Instant Pot on sauté, with vegetable broth, as needed throughout, sauté onion, celery and peppers. Stir. Add carrot and spices. Add rice. Stir. Add protein of choice. Stir for a few minutes. Add broth.

Close lid. On manual cook 4 min

Use natural release, then quick release

Remove lid, stir and adjust seasonings as needed

Zucchini Ravioli

This can be one of those recipes that you'll talk about long after. Who knew zucchini makes a good sub for noodles? I prefer it.

8 straight zucchini
Basil, parsley
Sliced tomatoes
3 cloves garlic, minced
Marinara sauce
1 pkg Beyond meat
1 onion, diced
Shredded vegan mozzarella

Brown beyond and onion. Mix with marinara sauce, basil, parsley and garlic. Slice zucchini lengthwise, thinly. In casserole lay out 2 pcs of zucchini like a cross. Put 1 Tbsp. of meat mixture in center, fold zucchini, and place seam side down in casserole dish. Continue until all zucchini is used up, and casserole is full in single layer. Put a slice of tomato on each zucchini ravioli, top with extra sauce if desired, and shredded cheese. Sprinkle with fresh basil.

Bake at 400* for 30 minutes. Serve with fresh bread

Chick'n Pot Pie

All of my favourites wrapped in a delicious flaky shell. Enough said.

6-8 mushrooms, diced
1 onion, diced
1 c of carrot, diced
3 ribs of celery, diced
3 cloves of garlic, minced
2 c cooked and cubed plant based chicken, or smoked tofu
¾ c of flour
1 c plant milk
1 c white wine
1 1/2 c vegetable broth
1 Tbsp. tamari
1 t Rosemary, thyme and sage
½ c each peas and corn
Salt and pepper
1 batch of pie pastry

Sauté vegetables over medium heat. Add flour and seasonings. Mix. Add wine, mix. Add milk and broth, mix. When thickened, turn to simmer. Roll out top and bottom of pie crust. Lay crust in pie dish. Fill with thickened pot pie mixture. Top with top pie pastry. Crimp or fold edges to close. Cut three triangles in top crust. Bake at 375* for 40 minutes until golden brown. Let sit 5 minutes.

Instant Pot Cincinnati Style Chili

A easy delicious meal that has many uses. It can be put on vegan hotdogs, over pasta, or just eaten with some yummy, crusty bread. Anyway you have it, it will be satisfying and delicious!

2 Tbsp. extra virgin olive oil
1 1/2 lb. beyond meat
1 large onion, minced
3 cloves of garlic, minced
2 Tbsp. of chili powder
½ tsp. Cayenne
2 tsp. dried oregano
2 tsp. of cocoa
½ tsp. allspice
½ tsp. ground cinnamon
½ tsp. of ground cloves
½ tsp. pepper
2 c tomato sauce
1 c vegetable broth
1 c water
2 Tbsp. apple cider vinegar
2 tsp. maple syrup

½ tsp. liquid smoke

In Instant Pot on sauté, add beef and onions. Add garlic and seasonings. Stir for 1 minute. Add in liquids and syrup. Stir. Put on sealing. Manual-20 minutes, allow timer to go to 20:00, naturally release pressure

BBQ'd Tofu

This recipe is so simple and makes a great main alongside mashed potatoes and veg of choice. Or it is equally comfortable nestled in between ciabatta buns with your favourite toppings.

Smoked tofu, sliced lengthways

Your favourite bbq sauce.

Brush bbq sauce on tofu and grill. Continue to brush and grill while flipping occasionally until the sauce is almost caramelized on the tofu. .

Beef Stroganoff

Sure to satisfy any palate, this is a go to main that satisfies most cravings for a rich, hearty meal. You can easily substitute the vegan burger for sautéed mushrooms and make this an equally delicious less processed, filling meal.

5 Tbsp. vegan butter

3 cloves garlic, minced

1 onion, chopped

1 3/4 - 2 cartons of a rich plant based milk like Oat Barista

Pepper to taste (I like mine with a bit more as I find it compliments the beefiness)

Parsley and salt to taste

4 Tbsp. of flour

1 pkg vegan ground (I used 6 'Beyond burgers)

Noodle of choice-cooked ahead

Cook burgers and break down. Once "meat" is browned, sprinkle with flour, stir until meat is cooked. Add veg broth and rich plant based milk of choice. Bring to light boil until thickened to desire texture, turn to low. Serve over pasta of choice with fresh bread.

Black Bean Quesadillas

A quick, delicious and healthy meal that comes together in under 20 minutes.

1 can of black beans
Garlic powder
Chopped fresh cilantro
Taco seasoning
Guacamole
Smoky Vegan cheddar cheese in misc. both as recipe ingredient, and for dipping
Salsa
Whole wheat tortillas

Drain black beans. Mash. Add red onion, 1 Tbsp. guacamole, 2 Tbsp. smoky cheddar sauce, Taco seasoning. Spread between 2 tortillas and grill in grill pan on medium until you get little grill marks on each side. Cut in quarters, serve with Pico de Gallo and smoky cheddar sauce

Tortiere

"Meat pie" with homemade pie pastry?! Yes please. It doesn't get any better than this. You can make this a lot healthier with whole wheat pie crust, and tvp...but as a once in a blue moon dinner.....you have to do it up in my opinion!

1 onion, chopped
3 cloves garlic, minced
4 mushrooms minced
1 c veg broth
3 Tbsp. cornstarch or 5 Tbsp. flour
½ c breadcrumbs
¾ tsp. salt
½ tsp. smoked paprika
2 Tbsp. tamari
½ tsp. dried thyme, sage, parsley
1/8 tsp. gr. cloves
1 pkg of 6 beyond burgers

Sauté onion, add meat, break down until crumbly, add herbs and seasonings.... stir with a bit of veg broth....thicken. Roll out dough, put in pie dish, add filling. Roll out top dough, place on filled pie...crimp or fork edges. If there is leftover pie pastry, I like to cut out shapes, and adhere them to the crust...turkey, cow...flowers etc...makes is fun!

Cut 3 vent holes.....400* bake 40 minutes or until golden. Let stand 10 minutes before slicing....I know it's hard to wait..., but trust me.

King Oyster Mushroom Scallops

These are a super impressive, I want to marry you sort of meal. I could just eat a plate of just these.....nothing else. That's all you need.....its mushroomgasmic. (Save the tops and ends for a lovely mushroom sauté.)

2 King Oyster mushrooms, ends removed, cut into scallop sized discs.

1 clove garlic, cut into 4 pcs

2 Tbsp. vegan butter

Sea salt

A little olive oil

Fresh Basil to taste

Dulse flakes- (optional)

Slice mushrooms scallop size. Heat cast iron pan. Sauté garlic until fragrant, with a little olive oil. Remove garlic, set aside. Add butter, raise to med, and when it melts add mushrooms...leave on same side for a few minutes to caramelize. Flip and repeat. Use any place you would use scallops...

Smoked Tofu Ciabatta's

I went out for lunch once and had the most satisfying vegan sandwich. This sandwich is my take on it. I have had meat eater's request seconds because it is so delicious. Make this and you won't be disappointed!

Smoked Tofu-Recipe in Misc.

Tamari

Cashew Mayo-Recipe in Misc.

Sliced Vegan Cheese-provolone or mature cheddar

Fresh spinach

Sliced Red Onion

Ciabatta buns

Slice tofu block into about 12pcs. Grill on both sides with a sprinkle of tamari. Set aside. Grill ciabatta buns on both top and bottom.

Spread cashew mayo on ciabatta buns. Put a slice of vegan cheese, and top with 3 or 4 pcs of grilled tofu. Add 4-5 spinach leaves and a couple rings of red onion. Top with ciabatta top.

These hold up extremely well made ahead. Wrap in parchment and tinfoil and store in fridge.

Loaded Coleslaw

I know this is technically a salad, but coleslaw is very filling. Throw in all your faves, drizzle with a little liquid gold (recipe in misc.), and sprinkle with some nooch! I like edamame, spinach, red onion, olives, and pickled radishes.

1 green cabbage

1 Taiwanese flat cabbage

1/4 of a red cabbage

1 red onion

1/2c sliced pickled radishes

½ c green olives

½ c edamame

A handful of spinach. Chopped

Smoked, grilled and cubed tofu, optional

In a large bowl, add half of the cabbage and the rest of the ingredients. Put the leftover cabbage in a bag for use later in the week. Mix in all ingredients in large bowl. Store in fridge.

Loaded Coleslaw Pitas

These are a delicious, healthy, easy sandwich alternative. Mix it up. Add sliced smoked and grilled tofu and you have yourself a meal!!

Whole Wheat pitas

Smoked, grilled tofu, sliced

Loaded coleslaw

Liquid gold

Grill pitas. Slice and stuff with the above. I sometimes make a few of these ahead and store them in the fridge for a quick snack!

Buddha Bowls

There was a time where my kids requested this weekly. A simple go to meal that uses up all kinds of different vegetables. It's the kind of meal you can empty your fridge with. Make a garlic guacamole for topping!

Base of choice-Rice or pasta

Different vegetables options are:

Edamame

Chopped Spinach

Diced Peppers

Diced red onion

Smoked tofu, cubed

Tomatoes, cored and chopped

Corn

Peas

Shredded carrot

Chopped green or black olives

Diced celery

Any other vegetable you can think of…..it's like a blank canvass, and you're the artist!

Make rice or pasta according to package directions. Prepare and chop all toppings, make guacamole.

Top rice or pasta as desired with any number of toppings!

Overnight Alfredo

I came up with this one night when I knew I had a lot of chores to do the next day. Super easy to throw together, then you blend the next day, pour it in a pot, and you'll have a delicious dinner in a jiffy!

In blender carafe add:
2 c cashews
Garlic powder
2 Tbsp. of Better than Bouillon paste
½ tsp. oregano
½ tsp. parsley
Salt to taste
8 c water
4 Tbsp. flour

Put all ingredients in blender carafe, put in fridge overnight. Blend in morn. Pour in pot, bring to a slow boil, simmer and thicken until desired texture is reached. Serve over your favourite pasta!

Taco Salad

This was one of our go-to meals when we first went plant-based. The tortilla chips are your canvas and the toppings are your paints! Make your own masterpiece!

Tortilla Chips

Black beans, mashed- (you can substitute any protein you want here)

Diced tomatoes

Diced Red Onion

Shredded Romaine, Spinach or Kale

Sliced Green or black olives

Chopped Cilantro

Easy cashew Queso- recipe in Apps

Vegan Sour Cream- recipe in Misc.

Violife shredded cheddar

Lay some tortilla chips on a plate, heat protein, and begin layering the different toppings over

the tortillas, in as much quantity as desired.
Enjoy!

Hungaloo

This was my Dad's recipe. He usually made it in the wee hours of the morn in a large electric skillet, like he had an uncontrollable craving he had to satisfy. It is basically a spaghetti casserole. The flavours amalgamate and it is even more delicious the next day!!

1 pkg Spagetinni broken in 1 ½" pcs

Olive oil or water for sautéing

Pasta Sauce of choice

1 pkg Beyond meat

1 Red pepper, diced

1 onion, diced

1 8oz pkg mushrooms, sliced

1 pkg spaghettini, broken in 2' pcs, cooked

Salt and pepper

Oregano, basil or Italian seasoning

Fresh garlic or garlic powder

Chop veg, cook pasta according until al dente. In large electric skillet, sauté onion until translucent. Add peppers and mushrooms. Sauté until broken down. Add beyond, and cook until browned. Add seasonings to desired taste. Add coioked pasta, mix well. Add pasta sauce and cook on low for ½ hour. Adjust seasonings. Enjoy with fresh bread.

Foccacia Pizza

Who needs take-out when you can whip up your own pizza! It's guaranteed to deliver!!

3-5 c Flour

2 1/4 tsp. Pizza Yeast

½ tsp. maple syrup

1 c warm water

½ tsp. salt

Olive oil for oiling

I like to make a "white' pizza....mix 1/4c olive oil with nooch, garlic powder, salt and oregano....brush on pizza dough and use this instead of traditional pizza sauce

Pizza sauce if using

vegan shredded mozzarella and cheddar cheese toppings of choice

In stand mixer bowl, proof yeast by mixing pizza yeast, water and maple syrup. Let bloom 10 minutes.

Add salt. Add flour in 1 c increments and turn on low to begin kneading. When dough pulls away from bowl, and it is clean of flour, it is ready. Remove dough from stand mixer bowl and put on floured surface temporarily. Put a tbsp. or 2 of olive oil in bottom of stand mixer bowl. Add dough, and flip to coat with oil.

Cover with towel, and let rise for 1 hour. When dough is risen, remove to floured surface and roll out with rolling pin to about ¼" thickness. Place on pizza stone and set aside for 10-20 minutes. Top as desired.

Bake for 15-20 minutes at 475*

Remove and let stand for 10 minutes.

Courage is the commitment to begin without any guarantee of success.

- Johann Wolfgang Von Goethe

Life can only be understood backwards, but it must be lived forwards.

- Soren Kierkegaard

Sometimes the bad things that happen in our lives put us directly on the path to the best things that will ever happen to us.

- Nicole Reed

Baked Goods

Baked Goods

These are the only recipes you need in the baked goods section. Trust me.....go to staples.

1. Quick Rise Bread
2. Homemade Foccacia
3. Hillbilly Hot Rolls

Quick-rise Bread

My youngest requests this frequently. It is so easy to make, I don't mind. This recipe normally makes 2 loaves of delicious carb-i-lish-os-ness, but I've doubled it here, and I put two rolls in the fridge to be baked after, because they don't last long!

6-7 c flour
6 tsp. yeast
4 c of warm water
2 tsp. of maple syrup
3 tsp. salt
½ c vegan butter, melted

If you know you want a savoury bread, you can add any herb at this point....garlic powder is a wonderful addition.

Proof yeast in mixing bowl with warm water and syrup. When bloomed, add butter, salt and flour a bit at a time. Spin until bowl is fairly clean and it's texture is ever so slightly sticky and elastic.

Add 1 T olive oil to dough ball in bowl, and roll around to coat all sides. Cover with towel 1 hour. Punch down, cut in 2 or 4 depending on whether or not you are using this recipe as doubled. Put in loaf pan. Rise 15-25 more minutes. You want it at least peeking over the top of your loaf pan. Bake at 375* for 25-30 minutes

Homemade Foccacia

This recipe can be your shape shifting recipe. It can be focaccia, it can be pizza, and it can be rolls. Just the time cooked will vary depending on what you're baking.

1Tbsp. olive oil reserved for rolling dough
Flavour paste: 4 Tbsp. olive oil, mixed with 1 tsp. each of garlic powder and oregano, and 1 Tbsp. nooch-set aside
2 ¼ tsp. yeast (I like the little jars of pizza yeast)
1 c warm water (not too hot or yeast won't bloom)
1 tsp. maple syrup (can use regular sugar, it's just my preference)
1 tsp. salt
(Mix yeast, warm water, and syrup in stand mixer bowl.....let it bloom.)
When bloomed add 1 t salt- mix.
Add ½ the flour. Mix on 2. Slowly mix in all the flour until fully incorporated. I usually like to mix an extra minute so the dough has more elasticity. Add 1 Tbsp. olive oil on dough ball. Roll

it around to coat it in oil. Cover bowl with towel, Let rise 1 hour.

If using like Foccacia, shape on stoneware rectangular pan and pat out until it's the same thickness throughout. Dimple surface with fingertips (this helps trap the deliciousness in the little grooves) Let rise 15-25 minutes in pan. Brush with flavour paste, top as desired. Can add pizza toppings here...or... keep it simple with sliced tomatoes, fresh spinach and red onion. Bake @ 450* for 15-20 minutes.

Hillbilly Hot Rolls

This is one of those recipes where people will be requesting it. It makes beautiful rolls to go along side any soup, pasta, or gravy recipe! Top with sugar, cinnamon and butter, and it is all of a sudden...dessert! (Increase the sugar if making as dessert)

2 1/4 tsp. pizza yeast

¼ c warm water

½ tsp. maple syrup

1 c warm plant milk

3 Tbsp. melted vegan butter

4 c flour

1 flax egg

1 tsp. garlic powder

1 tsp. salt

¼ c melted vegan butter for basting

In stand mixer bowl, proof yeast with water and syrup. Add rest of ingredients in stand mixer bowl. Mix until dough comes away from bowl clean. Over and let rise 1 hour. Punch down, remove from bowl. Tear off equal chunks, roll and place touching side by side on baking tray. Continue with dough until complete. Cover rolls on tray for 20 minutes. Bake @ 350* for 15 minutes until golden. Remove and brush with vegan butter.

Start where you are, use what you have, do what you can.

- Arthur Ashe

Be there for others, but never leave yourself behind.

- Dodinsky

When you get tired, learn to rest, not quit.
 - Banksy

DESSERTS

Desserts

1. Lemon Poppy Seed Bread 😇 😈
2. Easy Mug Cake 😇
3. Peanut Butter Cookies 😇
4. Really Good Oil Free Brownies 😇
5. 7 Layer Bars 😈
6. The Best Banana Bread 😇
7. Oatmeal Cookies 😇
8. Belle River Brownies 😈
10. Apple Crisp Tartlets 😈
11. Vegan Fudge 😈

Lemon Poppy Seed Bread

This is a classic, and one of my husband's faves. It doesn't get any better than this.

2 c flour
½ tsp. baking powder
½ tsp. salt
¾ tsp. sugar
1 c plant milk
¼ c juice and zest from those lemons
½ c apple sauce
1 tsp. poppy seeds

Topping:
1 c powdered sugar
4 tsp. lemon juice
1 tsp. zest

Preheat to 350. Mix dry, mix wet….mix wet and dry. Transfer to greased loaf pan. Bake 55 min or until top bounces back when lightly pressed.

Easy Mug Cake

This recipe is for when you're craving something sweet, but don't want to go through the hassle of making something elaborate. My youngest used to make it all the time.

In a coffee mug:

3 tsp. flour
¼ tsp. baking powder
2 Tbsp. cocoa powder
1 tsp. sugar
1 Tbsp. apple sauce
2 Tbsp. plant milk
2 Tbsp. water
½ tsp. vanilla

Add dry. Mix well, add wet, mix.
Put in micro for 1 minute, in 15 second intervals until fluffy.

Peanut Butter Cookies

I feel bad for people with a peanut allergy. Perhaps these could be made peanut free, but I've only tested it with peanut butter. These are delicious!

1 c peanut butter (I use organic)

½ C vegan butter

½ c flour

1 ½ c sugar, plus more for rolling

1 tsp. baking soda

1 tsp. baking powder

½ tsp. salt

Vanilla

1-3 Tbsp. plant milk if not holding together

Mix wet, mix dry, mix both together.

Roll in 1 tsp. balls, roll in sugar. Put on tray, flatten with fork. Bake for 16 minutes. Let cool.

Really Good Oil-Free Brownies

A fairly healthy dessert. You'll still want to go back for another.

1 c applesauce

1 ½ tsp. vanilla

1 ½ tsp. apple cider vinegar

¾ c flour

1 c maple syrup

1 tsp. cornstarch

2 tsp. baking powder

½ tsp. baking soda

3 T cocoa powder

½ tsp. salt

½ tsp. cinnamon

½ c vegan chocolate chips

1/3 c walnuts (optional)

350* Mix wet, mix dry, mix both. Pour into pan. Bake 25-30 minutes. The top should be slightly firm.

7 Layer Bars

Addictive. A great pot luck recipe.

1 ½ c graham crumbs

½ c vegan butter (mix these two ingredients, and press into 9 x 13 non-stick pan. in layers....

1 c crisped rice (use chocolate for a different flavour)

1 c. dark chocolate chips

1 c maple bits

1 1/3 c coconut

1 c chopped pecans

1 can of sweetened condensed coconut milk poured over all. Bake 350* for 25-30 minutes

The Best Banana Bread

Who doesn't love a moist banana bread? Slather with a little plant based butter, and you have yourself breakfast with a nice cup of coffee.

In blender mix everything but flour:

2 large really ripe bananas (got brown mushy bananas no one will eat? This is the recipe you save them for!)

2 flax eggs

1 tsp. vanilla

1 c sugar

4 tsp. baking powder

½ tsp. salt

Vegan Chocolate chips

2 c flour

350* spritz loaf pan or line muffin tins

Mix in chips. Pour into loaf pan-bake 45-55 min or until toothpick comes clean

Or, put in muffin tins, bake 20-35 minutes or until toothpick comes clean. Serve with coconut cool whip

Oatmeal Cookies

Tastes like biting into a memory. I like mine a little crunchier, so I cook them a bit longer.

1 c applesauce
2 c sugar
1 tsp. vanilla
2 flax eggs
1 tsp. each of baking powder/baking soda
½ tsp. salt
2 c oats
1 ½ c coconut
Water to moisten

Mix wet, mix dry. Mix together. Moisten with water. Put on baking sheet, flatten with fork. Bake @ 375* for 30 to 40 minutes

Belle River Brownies

This is my homage to a little bakery in the town of Belle River Ont. They had the most deliciously moist, fudgy vegan brownies ever. They were so rich. I'm trying to capture that with this recipe.

1 whole dark choc bar (400g)
1 stick plus ½ stick vegan butter
½ c olive oil
2 c flour
½ c cocoa
½ tsp. baking powder
1 tsp. salt
1 ½ c sugar
Flax eggs x 4
vanilla

9 x 13 375* Mix dry. Mix chocolate (melt it) butter and oil. Stir in flax egg. Mix all. Press into 9 x 13 pan. Bake 38 minutes, edges should feel firm and almost crusty. Freeze for 1 hour. Store in fridge

Apple Crisp Tartlets

I created this one day when craving nostalgia. It is a mix between apple pie and apple crisp.

1 batch of pie pastry (recipe in misc.)
7 apples, cored and chopped
½ c sugar
½ c brown sugar
2 Tbsp. flour
1 tsp. cinnamon
1 Tbsp. lemon juice
1 flax egg

Streusel Topping:
½ c flour, ¼ c brown sugar, 4 Tbsp. melted vegan butter, ¼ c rolled oats, 1/8 tsp. salt- mix all

Start by chopping apples. In a large bowl add all ingredients except pastry and mix. Roll out pie pastry. Cut out circles until all pastry is used up, press in stoneware muffin tins. Add apple pie filling. Top with streusel topping.

Bake @ 425* for 20 minutes, turn down to 375* bake for 25 minutes. Remove and cool. Serve with coconut whipped cream or vegan ice cream.

Vegan Fudge

A delicious dessert, that is incredibly easy to throw together! You'll make it again and again......

400 g of dark chocolate

1 can of sweetened condensed coconut milk

1 c of chopped nuts of choice (optional) - I like cashews

Coarse salt (optional)

In a double boiler, add chocolate and condensed coconut milk, Stir until melted and mix in nuts if using.

Pour into a parchment lined 8 x 8 casserole, top with a sprinkling of coarse salt if using. Cover and store in fridge for about 4 hours.

Remove and cube. Keep in fridge.

When things do not go your way, remember that every challenge-every adversity-contains within it the seeds of opportunity and growth.

-Roy T. Bennett

The problem is not the problem. The problem is your attitude about the problem.

- Jack Sparrow

Eat to live, not live to eat.

- Benjamin Franklin

Breakfast

Breakfast

1. Homemade Cashew Milk
2. Tofu fried bacon
3. Tasty Egg Mix
4. Mung Bean Omelet
5. Vegan Pancakes
6. Vegan Hollandaise
7. Vegan Dippin' Egg
8. Tofu Breakfast stack
9. Homemade Bagels
10. Veggie Benedict

Homemade Oat Milk

Whomever said milk only comes from cows was wrong. Turns out, you can make a pretty good facsimile with cashews. It's got a nice creaminess, without the dairy.

1 ½ c. raw cashews

8 c. water

Pinch of salt

A drizzle of maple syrup

Blend in a very good blender. Strain through nutjug three times for extra filtered.

Tofu fried bacon

The thinner you slice this, the crispier it becomes. Dip it in syrup and it is so delicious! Reminds me of bacon.....but no pigs were harmed in the making of this.

1 pkg extra firm smoked tofu, sliced thin.

Marinate with:

1/3 c tamari

2 tsp. balsamic

3 Tbsp. maple syrup

3 tsp. liquid smoke

1 tsp. nutritional yeast

Grill slices on medium heat until browned. I like mine dipped in syrup.

Tasty Egg Mix

This recipe mimics the flavour and texture of egg yolk well. Pour it on scrambled tofu, or dip tofu slices in it, fry them up and see for yourself.

1 c nutritional yeast
½ c of potato starch
6 Tbsp. tapioca starch
1 tsp. baking powder
1 tsp. baking soda
½ tsp. black salt
½ tsp. onion powder
Pinch of turmeric

Put all in jar, mix. Store in dark place. When ready to use, mix 3 T with a little bit of water and pour over crumbled tofu.

Mung Bean Omelet

If this is done right, it is really close to eggs. Regardless, it's delicious with vegan cheese.

1 c mung beans
½ tsp. black salt plus ¼ tsp.
¼ t each of garlic and onion powder
Pepper to taste
¼ tsp. turmeric
1 Tbsp. olive oil
1-1 ¼ c plant milk

Soak mung beans overnight. Drain. Add to blender with rest of ingredients. Blend 1 minute, Blend again. Should be smooth and fluffy. Add 1 t baking powder blend again. Grease a cast iron pan. Turn heat to medium. Once hot, add ladleful of mung mixture. Cover with lid. Cook 1-3 minutes, once edges are dry, flip. Stuff as desire, fold and warm

Vegan Pancakes

A constant request in my home, and sometimes we have it for dinner. Top it with maple syrup, chopped pecans and sliced bananas and it becomes a decadent meal, whether for breakfast or dinner!

2 c flour

2 Tbsp. sugar

1 Tbsp. baking powder

½ tsp. salt

¼ c of melted butter or applesauce

Flax eggs-2

2 c plant milk

Mix all. Heat cast iron pan to medium. Grease. Pour a ladleful of batter in pan. When edges begin to look cooked, flip. Cook 1-2 minutes more.

Vegan Hollandaise

What is richer than delicious buttery hollandaise dripping over perfectly toasted crumpets topped with tofu and vegan bacon or sausage? An impressive start to the day!

½ c cashews
2 c plant milk
1/2 c nooch
Pinch of turmeric
Pinch of smoked paprika
1 tsp. both onion and garlic powder
2 Tbsp. lemon juice
1 Tbsp. cornstarch mixed with 2 Tbsp. water

Blend all. Pour in pot, taste and adjust. Bring to heat to thicken a bit. Remove from heat immediately. Serve over English muffins topped with tofu and vegan bacon or sausage or go with tomato and guacamole.

Vegan Dipping Egg

I found this recipe online and adapted it. A perfect vegan breakfast sauce for dipping toast!

1 c water

1 Tbsp. plus ½ tsp. cornstarch

2 Tbsp. olive oil

2 Tbsp. nooch

¼ tsp. Black salt

¼ tsp. turmeric

In a small saucepan, whisk together cornstarch and water. Stir in rest, cook over medium heat until thickened. Remove immediately. Serve with plant-buttered toast.

Tofu Breakfast Stacks

A delicious stack of tofu utilizing tasty egg mix. Nestled between the layers, is sautéed mushrooms, onions, and vegan cheddar cheese. Almost like a breakfast lasagna. Yum.

Block of extra firm tofu

8 oz mushrooms, sliced

1 onion, diced

Slice mushrooms and dice onion. Sauté until cooked, remove.

3 Tbsp. Tasty egg mixture with 3 Tbsp. of water, mix.

Slice tofu lengthwise into thin slices. Cut each slice in half. Dip in tasty egg mixture, fry on both sides.

Stack tofu, with a Tbsp. of mushroom, onion mixture. Top with vegan cheese of choice. Top with another slice of tofu. Place mushroom, onion, cheese mixture on top.

Place a 3rd tofu slice on with mushrooms onions and cheese.

Bake @ 350* until cheese is melted.

Get out your knife and fork, and enjoy!

Homemade Bagels

You don't need to go to your local bakery to have fresh bagels at home. With a little effort, you can have a delicious breakfast that's great for a relaxing morning, or on the go!!

For the dough:

1 ½ c warm water

3 t. quick rise yeast

1 tsp. brown sugar or maple syrup

4 c flour

2 tsp. salt

For boiling the bagels:

8 c water

1 tsp. baking soda

For topping bagels:

Sesame seeds, poppy seeds, or everything bagel seasoning, garlic powder and nutritional yeast.

Make dough by proofing yeast in stand mixer bowl with warm water and brown sugar or maple syrup. Let sit 10 minutes. Yeast should be foamy, If it's not, it's likely old.

Once proofed mix in flour and salt. Let stand mixer run for 5 minutes. Dough will form ball, and sides of the bowl fairly clean when it's ready. Remove dough to floured surface and oil bowl. Put dough back in and flip to coat. Cover and rise for 1 hour.

Once dough has risen, punch down, and turn out onto floured surface. Divide into 8-10 pcs. Roll into long pencil shape, and then form to make circle. Join and press ends together. Place on parchment lined sheet. Fill pot with water, and bring to boil. Drop bagels in a couple at a time. Flip in water, leave for 1 minute, and remove with slotted spoon to baking sheet. Sprinkle with desired seeds. Bake @ 400* for 25 minutes. Remove and cool. They will firm op as they cool.

The way I see it, if you want the rainbow, you got to put up with the rain.
 - Dolly Parton

Strength is keeping it together, when everyone expects you to fall apart.

- Paul Coelho

> It is often the small steps, not the giant leaps that bring about the most lasting change.
>
> - HRM Queen Elizabeth II

Miscellaneous

Miscellaneous

1. Smoked tofu
2. Smoky cheddar cheese sauce
3. Cashew Mayo
4. Liquid gold
6. Sundried tomato bacon
7. Pickled radishes
8. Pie Pastry
9. Pico de Gallo
10. Simple Sour Cream
11. Sandy's Slatherin' sauce
12. Vegan Worcestershire
13. Flax egg

Smoked tofu

I could not have a vegan recipe book without having a recipe for smoked tofu. During Covid, my favourite tofu brand stopped selling smoked tofu....a delight because it can be made into so many things. So, I was forced to try and smoke it myself.....without a smoker. I came up with this.....an incredible recipe to have in your repertoire. You'll come back to it time and time again.

Extra Firm Tofu

Tamari

Liquid smoke

Smoked paprika

Take extra firm tofu. Put it casserole dish. Drizzle with tamari. A few drops of liquid smoke. A couple pinches of smoked paprika Flip and repeat.

300* oven for 1 ½ hours-....flipping 1/2 way through. (The longer you cook it, the firmer and more like chicken it tastes, except you're not harming a cute little chicken, your just eating a bean!) Remove and cool. Grill and use anytime you need a meaty substitute, its great on sandwiches!!!

Smoky Cheddar Cheese Sauce

This one goes well with tacos, vegan nachos, or anyplace you want to use a cheesy sauce. If you have any leftovers, you can make a nice cheesy soup out of it.

6 potatoes, chopped

2 carrots, chopped

1 c raw cashews

1 tsp. salt

Put in pot, cover with water. Bring to boil. Cook until potatoes and carrots are soft. Drain, put in blender. To the mixture add:

1 Tbsp. smoked paprika

1 Tbsp. salt

1 c nooch

Blend. Taste and adjust. Serve with nachos or with tortilla chips,

Cashew Mayo

You don't need a sauce made with eggs to kick up flavour! And because it is made with nuts, you can use it in place of mayo and it will hold up for any picnic recipe!

A fantastic recipe to have in your repertoire…..use anywhere you'd use mayo!

3 c. Cashews

2½ c. water

½ tsp. salt

Blend until smooth. Use in place of mayo.

Liquid Gold

This dressing is made with flax oil for health. The components in flax comprise our cell walls! Amazing! This is my go to dressing for almost any salad I have. Serve with loaded coleslaw and it makes for an incredibly healthy meal!

In jar or bottle....fill with....

¾ flax oil

¼ lemon Juice

1 Tbsp. garlic powder

¼ c nooch

1 Tbsp. sumac

2 tsp. of salt

½ tsp. herb of choice- I like oregano

Put in mason jar, shake.

Sundried Tomato Bacon

I created this one day because I noticed that sundried tomatoes have a very chewy, bacon like texture. So I thought, why not add a little bacon flavour?

Sundried Tomatoes

Liquid smoke

Tamari

Smoked paprika

Cut sundried tomatoes in small pieces. In bowl drizzle with a bit of tamari, liquid smoke, and smoked paprika. Bake @ 170* until dry.

Pickled Radishes

A great accompaniment to sandwiches, and in the loaded coleslaw recipe in this book, it will be something you always want to have in your fridge.

3 bags of radishes, sliced

Jar to fit

Fill jar with ¾ vinegar

¼ water ratio

Pour liquid from jar in a pot with a couple of bay leaves, bring to a boil

Stick in a couple bay leaves. After boiling a couple minutes, pour over radishes and let cool before putting in fridge.

Pie Pastry

This will be your go to for baked goods, both savoury and sweet. When the pastry is homemade, you know whatever is in it is going to be delicious...... Don't lose this one! Makes one top and one bottom.

2 c flour
2 Tbsp. sugar- omit if using for savoury purposes
8 Tbsp. vegan butter
2 Tbsp. applesauce or olive oil
3 Tbsp. water

Mix all in stand mixer. Remove dough. Separate into 2 equal balls. Wrap with plastic wrap and cool in fridge 1 hour. Remove and use as recipe directs.

Pico De Gallo

I remember going to Mexico one year, and they had this alongside their brunch buffet. You put it on everything. So fresh and with a slight citrus flavour, it is a great accompaniment to anything Mexican.

2 c tomatoes, cored and diced
¼ c red onion, diced
½ jalapeno, seeded and diced
1 Tbsp. garlic, minced
Juice of 2 lemons
1/4c cilantro, chopped

Mix all. Let sit in fridge a few hours to establish flavours.

Simple vegan sour cream

So easy, you just need a good blender.

1 ½ c cashews

2 Tbsp. Lemon juice

2 tsp. apple cider vinegar

½ tsp. salt

¼ tsp. garlic powder

½ tsp. dijon

½ tsp. cream of tartar

½ c-1 c water

Blend until smooth and creamy.

Sandy's Slatherin' Sauce

Homage to my Mom. I got this recipe from her. I think she adapted it from a famous BBQ place in my hometown. It's always a hit and is great slathered on everything.

½ c ketchup-I like French's
½ c mustard-same as above
½ c vinegar
½ tsp. salt and pepper
½ tsp. garlic powder
¼ c sugar
½-2 tsp. cayenne
½ tsp. chili powder
¼ tsp. onion powder

Mix. Let stand. Test. Adjust.

Vegan Worcestershire

Every once and a while you run into a recipe that calls for Worcestershire. Well here is a great vegan version.

6 Tbsp. apple cider vinegar
2 Tbsp. tamari
1 Tbsp. brown sugar
2 tsp. prepared mustard
¼ tsp. onion and garlic powder
¼ tsp. cinnamon
Dash of cayenne and chili powder
Dash of allspice
Salt to taste
Whisk with a ¼ c water
Store in fridge

Flax Egg

I don't know who came up with this concoction, but it is a vegan staple in many dishes, as it mimics eggs in baking. This recipe makes one flax egg. Multiply as needed in your recipes.

1 Tbsp. ground flax

1 Tbsp. water

Mix. Let sit a few minutes to thicken. Use as desired.

Dear Reader,

There isn't a moment that goes by in my everyday where I wish that I was not afflicted with MS.

Although this journey has been hard as hell.....at the same time, a large part of me knows that if I had to live this life all over again.....I wouldn't change a thing.

MS has opened my eyes to the things that are truly important in life.....and I hope my book reflects that.

Fight on, warriors.

Nicole Tracey
April 113th, 2024

,

References

https://cmhahkpr/importance-of-self-care/

Nicole Tracey is an author, vegan foodie and lover of animals.

She studied nutrition at the Canadian School of Natural Nutrition and is a writer for www.msfitnesschallenge.org.

She enjoys cooking, feeling the sun on her skin, and spending time with family.

She lives with her husband, and three sons in Prince Edward Island, Canada.